FOCUS ON

ADVENTURES IN ODYSSEY®

CANDID CONVERSATIONS WITH CONNIE, VOL 3

KATHY BUCHANAN

Tyndale House Publishers, Inc.
Carol Stream, Illinois

Candid Conversations with Connie, Vol. 3:
A Girl's Guide to Entertainment, Body Image, and Social Media
© 2015 Focus on the Family

A Focus on the Family book published by
Tyndale House Publishers, Inc., Carol Stream, Illinois 60188

Focus on the Family and *Adventures in Odyssey* and the accompanying logos and designs are federally registered trademarks of Focus on the Family, 8605 Explorer Drive, Colorado Springs, CO 80920.

TYNDALE and Tyndale's quill logo are registered trademarks of Tyndale House Publishers, Inc.

No part of this publication may be reproduced, stored in a retrieval system, or transmitted in any form or by any means—electronic, mechanical, photocopy, recording, or otherwise—without prior written permission of Focus on the Family.

All Scripture quotations, unless otherwise marked, are taken from the *Holy Bible, New International Version*®. NIV®. Copyright © 1973, 1978, 1984 by Biblica, Inc.® Used by permission of Zondervan. All rights reserved worldwide *(www.zondervan.com)*. The "NIV" and "New International Version" are trademarks registered in the United States Patent and Trademark Office by Biblica, Inc.™

Scripture quotations marked (2011) are taken from the *Holy Bible, New International Version*®. NIV®. Copyright © 1973, 1978, 1984, 2011 by Biblica, Inc.® Used by permission of Zondervan. All rights reserved worldwide *(www.zondervan.com)*. The "NIV" and "New International Version" are trademarks registered in the United States Patent and Trademark Office by Biblica, Inc.™

Scripture quotations marked (KJV) are taken from the *King James Version*.

Scripture quotations marked (NASB) are taken from the *New American Standard Bible*®. Copyright © 1960, 1962, 1963, 1968, 1971, 1972, 1973, 1975, 1977, 1995 by The Lockman Foundation. Used by permission. *(www.Lockman.org)*.

Scripture quotations marked (NCV) are taken from the *Holy Bible, New Century Version*, copyright © 1987, 1988, 1991 by Thomas Nelson, Inc.. Used by permission. All rights reserved.

Scripture quotations marked (ESV) are taken from the *Holy Bible, English Standard Version*, copyright © 2001 by Crossway, a publishing ministry of Good News Publishers. Used by permission. All rights reserved.

Scripture quotations marked (NLT) are taken from the *Holy Bible, New Living Translation*, copyright © 1996, 2004, 2015 by Tyndale House Foundation. Used by permission of Tyndale House Publishers, Inc., Carol Stream, Illinois 60188. All rights reserved.

The use of material from or references to various websites does not imply endorsement of those sites in their entirety. Availability of websites and pages is subject to change without notice.

Cover design by Beth Sparkman
Interior design by Lexie Rhodes
Illustrations by Gary Locke
Interior laptop drawing copyright © SpiffyJ/iStockphoto. All rights reserved.

Library of Congress Cataloging-in-Publication Data for this title can be found at www.loc.gov.

ISBN 978-1-58997-798-3

For manufacturing information regarding this product, please call 1-800-323-9400.

Printed in the United States of America

21 20 19 18 17 16 15
7 6 5 4 3 2 1

For my daughter Bella.
When God gave you to me, He gave me pure joy wrapped up in a little girl. I love your enthusiasm, your always grateful heart, and the wonder you have for every day of life. You spread encouragement to everyone around you. What a gift you have! And what a gift you are to us.

Contents

Introduction 1

Chapter One: Chasing a Green-Footed Chipmunk 5
    (True Beauty)

Chapter Two: Congratulations! You Made Dust Today 19
    (Eating Well)

Chapter Three: How to Avoid Being Attacked by a Toaster 39
    (bYOUtiful)

Chapter Four: Lesson from a Thirty-Four-Pound,
        Pink Rhinoceros 55
    (Careful What You Buy Into)

Chapter Five: Lesson from a Marshmallow 67
    (Waiting for Better)

Chapter Six: The Gift of Toothpaste 81
    (Great Attitude=Gratitude)

Chapter Seven: Careful with Those Hedge Trimmers! 97
    (Being Smart Online)

CONTENTS

Chapter Eight: When You're Just Like a Shaken Can of Coke 111
(Think Before You Post)

Chapter Nine: Aaaack! Look at Me! 129
(Texting Troubles)

Chapter Ten: Chickens on a Keyboard 139
(Cyberbullying Stinks)

Chapter Eleven: Remote-Controlled Adventures 151
(Media Choices)

Chapter Twelve: Drowning in Honey 163
(The Time of Your Life)

Notes 183

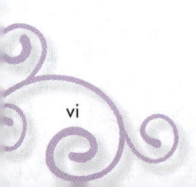

Introduction

"How about *Digging for Destruction*?" Camilla asks. "It got great reviews."

"Seriously?" Tamika says, rolling her eyes. "The movie's about giant moles out for revenge against mankind."

Penny slurps her milkshake. "I thought it was possums out for payback."

"Whatever," Olivia replies. "Who would want to watch rodents taking over the world? Can't we see something more romantic—like *Moonlight over Paris*? My Facebase friends have raved about it!"

Emily scans a webpage on her tablet. "But the critics' reviews have been awful. I mean, it's about a man who falls in love with a dog washer because she trimmed his poodle so well. Boring."

"And a poodle isn't even that hard to trim," Penny pipes up. "Have you ever tried grooming a llama? Now I could fall in love with someone who could do that."

"Well, sounds like it's between a well-trimmed poodle and a malicious mole," Katrina says.

"Or possum," Emily adds.

I'm Connie Kendall, and I'm listening to a typical Saturday-night discussion. The conversation might not always be about revenge-filled rodents or romance spurred on by clipping shears, but it's usually about deciding which movie we're going to watch on our Girls' Movie Night. We always meet at Whit's End to have a snack and discuss which movie to see. After all, a girl can't live on popcorn and Milk Duds alone . . . although that is a pretty good start.

We're crammed into a booth with our smartphones and tablets, checking movie times and reviews. Emily's shooting a selfie. Penny's texting Wooton. Katrina's on some webpage. Camilla and Olivia are looking for recommendations on social-media sites. Tamika's listening to music. And I'm trying to make sure my milkshake doesn't spill all over their devices.

"Can't we just decide on a movie ourselves, instead of going online?" I ask, interrupting the chatter.

The girls look at me blankly.

"I mean, it feels like it should be simpler than all this. I just want to spend time with you guys. I don't need all this . . . noise."

"Sorry, I'll turn down my ringer," Penny says, adjusting her phone.

"Not that kind of noise," I say. "I mean the noise of all this information. Media everywhere giving us news and opinions—like what to wear, watch, and listen to."

"But we're going to a movie," Olivia says. "That's media too."

"I know," I say. "We can't escape it."

"Kinda like the mole that's taking over the world," Camilla says. "I mean possum."

"Well, I think it's convenient," Emily says. "I like having reviews and movie times on my phone."

"I like that too," I say. "But not when it becomes so consuming. There has to be some kind of balance."

"Uh, Miss Kendall?" Eugene interrupts as he approaches our booth. "Isn't your show starting soon?"

I spin around to look at the clock. My talk show *Candid Conversations with Connie* is supposed to start in five minutes!

"But . . . I don't even know what my topic is," I blurt.

"I think you might," Katrina says, pushing her glasses up the bridge of her nose. "You could talk about the media and its influence on us."

"We could touch on technology, too." Emily says.

The other girls nod in agreement.

"But I'm not prepared," I say. "You're all going to have to help me."

The girls quickly jump up and parade behind me into the studio.

I think it's going to be a pretty interesting show. Maybe you'd like to join us!

CHAPTER 1

Chasing a Green-Footed Chipmunk

True Beauty

The movie the girls and I ended up seeing last week was intense. You know the kind . . . You get so drawn in that you reach for a soda and drink half of it before you realize it's not even yours. Then the guy in the next seat glares at you because you just finished off his Dr Pepper. *Oops.* Anyway, the movie starred one of my favorite actresses: the stunning Elsie Briggs.

Elsie is beautiful and talented. In the movie, she played a karate expert and brilliant scientist who marches into the White

House to fight off thirty-seven aliens who have taken over the United States. Her only weapons are her wits and her martial-arts expertise. And you wouldn't believe how she uses a metal spatula to defend herself against the nine-armed monsters.

I sat on the edge of my seat as a final explosion demolished the building, throwing our heroine several hundred feet onto the White House lawn. But just when I thought it was over for poor Elsie, she slowly stood up and brushed herself off. Her hair was adorably disheveled. A cute black smudge streaked her cheek. If anything, fighting aliens only made her look *more* beautiful. Flashing a determined smile, she ran back to the smoke-blackened scene to battle the final alien.

This woman just survived an alien attack and an explosion, and she looked better than I do after half an hour of primping. *Why can't I look like that?* I wondered.

Here's the thing: Elsie Briggs doesn't even look like Elsie Briggs. Nor do any of the musicians, movie stars, or models you see.

Really.

The actresses and models who appear in magazines and on TV screens receive hours of professional beauty treatment. Their faces get contoured with cosmetic shading. Their best features are enhanced. Their hair is colored and highlighted. A stylist teases, curls, and pins the perfect hairstyle. Hairpieces are even added to make their hair appear fuller.

When a model gets on set for a photo shoot, fans and lighting are arranged to create the best possible appearance. Of the hundreds—or even thousands—of photos taken, only the top one is selected and then adjusted using Photoshop. Skin blemishes are erased, eyebrows lifted, cheekbones raised, lips plumped, legs and waistlines minimized. By the time the photo is printed in a magazine, you might not even recognize the model if she stood in line in front of you at the candy store . . . because *she doesn't really look like that.*

So if you had all the money in the world, you could hire a staff of people to make you look movie-star perfect all the time too. But really, how would they all fit in the back of your mom's minivan? And remember: makeup runs and hair goes flat. So your "perfection" would be fake and fleeting.

After the movie, we headed to Whit's End and ended up talking about our desire to look like women who don't exist.

"I'm discouraged," Tamika said, stirring her milkshake. "Even though I know what I'm seeing in movies and magazines isn't real, I still look in the mirror and feel . . . I don't know . . . I'm just not pretty enough."

The other girls murmured that they felt the same way. That made me sad. My friends are beautiful, healthy, vivacious young women like you. They don't need to change their appearance at all! But that's not what the media communicates to them.

Penny fiddled with her napkin. "Yeah, trying to be beautiful is like chasing a green-footed chipmunk."

All eyes immediately turned to her.

"What was that?" I asked.

She explained . . .

Penny's Story

Last Saturday I spent half the day helping Wooton catch a chipmunk. Wooton had been painting some furniture green—he's all about going green, y'know—and the chipmunk ran through his paint tray and into his house.

By the time I came over, the little critter had left green footprints all over the kitchen floor, the stairway, and the rocket-shaped shower stall.

"There's nothing harder to catch than a green-footed chipmunk," Wooton told me as he invited me to join the chase.

I went to the garage, grabbed his fishing net, and

threw myself into catching the little guy. He was so quick and agile that it took us two hours and two pounds of peanuts to finally coax him back outside!

Wooton thought catching a chipmunk was hard, but as I ran around his house, I kept thinking how elusive the world's standard of beauty can be. You can't really keep up with it, and you won't ever catch it—especially in a couple of hours.

Penny made a good point. (I think.) To clarify what she was saying, I asked, "So what's considered beautiful is always changing?"

"Exactly," she said. "When I began studying art history, I was struck by the curviness of the women in older paintings. They were a whole lot heavier than the models you see in magazines today. Yet, at that time, *those* were the women considered beautiful. *Those* were the women that others aspired to look like. They looked healthy and full of energy."

I nodded in agreement. "Isn't it funny that society's opinion of beauty doesn't stay the same?"

Penny smiled. "I can't wait until scrawny people with pointy elbows and knobby knees become all the rage. Then *I'll* be a supermodel."

Changing Standards

A few centuries back, women who were curvy and pale were considered extremely attractive. Thin women were viewed as malnourished servants. Full-figured females appeared wealthy and well fed. Their pale skin meant these women had the privilege of staying inside. Working women toiled in the field, growing tan in the sun.

In the early 1900s, this started to change as working women found themselves indoors, growing pale in factories and offices. Then tanned skin became more desirable.

Trends in fashion and style change more frequently than the ice-cream flavors at Whit's End. The "in" colors switch each season. Pixie hairstyles change to long, flowing waves. Thin, arched eyebrows switch to fuller brows. Natural-look makeup transitions to over-the-top, bold colors. Waiflike arms replace toned, muscular arms as the ideal look.

Trying to chase down the perfect weight, shape, hair color, and eyebrow arch *is* like trying to catch a green-footed chipmunk. It's impossible. Yet most of us strive to become whatever the rest of the world sees as beautiful—even though the "in" look is constantly changing and is often unobtainable.

Here's a Secret...

Every woman—no matter how gorgeous she appears to be—wants to change something about herself. That's why women spend $12 *billion* each year on plastic surgery.[1] They're chasing an impossible ideal that's more difficult to catch than Wooton's green-footed chipmunk.

A girl named Brittany from Scranton, Pennsylvania, recently contacted me after hearing my radio show. I think you'll relate to her question . . .

Q: It feels like you have to be pretty to be well liked or even noticed. I hate all the pressure to be beautiful and skinny. What can I do?
#CandidConversationsWithConnie

We're all victims of the beauty pursuit. And Brittany is right: pretty people get more attention. At some point in your life, a boy will notice you simply because he finds you pretty. Outward appearances *do* matter in the world we live in.

While there's nothing wrong with putting some effort into looking your best, you are far more than what you see in the mirror. At your very core, you need to believe that you're a perfect creation of your heavenly Father. Your value is so much more significant than your weight, your hairstyle, or what you wear. You wouldn't buy a house without touring the inside, even if the exterior was perfect. You wouldn't purchase a red convertible without giving it a test drive to make sure the engine works. What's inside matters a *lot*.

So you have a choice. You can . . .

A. work hard on having a shiny exterior or
B. make an effort to build godly character and grow closer to God.

Plenty of people choose A. They might get a lot of attention at first, but when your looks become the priority, things like deep friendships and meaningful conversation can often take a backseat.

When we choose B, we don't worry as much about people's first impressions. We're more interested in having friends who know us well, who enjoy who we are, and who are kind and loyal. We'd rather spend less time on our hair and more time having fun with friends, getting to know God better, and developing our talents and interests.

Receiving attention for what we wear to school isn't attention that lasts. The Bible says it best (it usually does): "Charm is deceptive, and beauty is fleeting; but a woman who fears the Lord is to be praised" (Proverbs 31:30).

My grandmother was a remarkable woman. Her life wasn't always easy. She didn't have a lot of money. She never appeared in movies or on magazine covers. But when she passed away several years ago, her funeral was packed. I'll never forget how many people walked up to me and said, "Your grandma was so beautiful."

I nodded because I knew what they meant. Grandma had wiry, gray hair and a face full of wrinkles and creases. She was a little chunky, and her skin sagged. But she glowed with joy. She loved God and knew He loved her. Her bright eyes shone with wisdom and compassion. Her smile lit up a room. Her laugh made others laugh. She was simply . . . stunning.

Do you like hanging out with your best friend because she has perfectly plucked eyebrows or because she treats you with kindness and stands up for you? Do you like your favorite teacher because she wears the latest hairstyle or because she's funny and encouraging?

The Bible reminds us that beauty isn't an outward quality. True beauty comes from within—from the quality of our spirits. First Peter 3:3-4 (NLT) says,

> *Don't be concerned about the outward beauty of fancy hairstyles, expensive jewelry, or beautiful clothes. You should clothe yourselves instead with the beauty that comes from within, the unfading beauty of a gentle and quiet spirit, which is so precious to God.*

The Bible doesn't forbid us from wearing earrings and styling our hair. It does say to *not be concerned* about those things. Don't fret over looking perfect. Don't use your time standing in front of the mirror preening and primping. Instead, clothe yourself with the beauty that comes from within. That's where we should focus our attention . . . on being beautiful *inside*.

As I read through 1 Peter a few months ago, that verse really impacted me. To be honest, I've struggled with that whole "gentle and quiet" bit. I'm about as quiet and gentle as a camel in a glass museum. So I memorized that verse and tried living it out in my actions.

One day I went into Whit's End and hardly said a word. It nearly killed me. I had stories I wanted to tell, songs I wanted to sing, and questions I wanted to ask. I bit my tongue so much to keep from blurting things out that it swelled to three times its normal size. Finally, when I thought I would absolutely explode (and it was only ten in the morning!), Whit asked me, "What's wrong? Why are you being so quiet today?"

So I told him about the verse.

Do you know what he did? He *laughed*.

"Connie," he said, "the word *quiet* in that verse actually means 'peaceful.' A woman who is at peace doesn't argue, gossip, start fights, or complain. She spreads life and goodness, like you do when you interact with the kids and tell your stories. Sometimes peace can sound a lot like loud laughter."

"Really?" I said. "So do you think I'm beautiful on the inside?"

Whit smiled. "Connie, I think your insides are stunning."

Thankfully I had the rest of the day to make up for my quiet morning. Even with my swollen tongue, I managed to get in my daily allotment of words. And I'll never forget Whit's words to me.

Outward beauty is fleeting. Your youthful appearance is temporary. And no matter how pretty you are, it will only take you so far. Beauty matters just a bit. It's like the cherry on the sundae. You might notice it when Whit hands you a treat across the counter, but ultimately the chocolate, caramel, and ice cream matter a whole lot more. Oh . . . and the whipped cream. That's the life-changing part. (Suddenly I'm feeling really hungry.)

Anyway, I don't want to settle for outside beauty that only the world can see. I want to be beautiful . . . for *God*. I want others to see His grace and compassion through me. I want God to be honored by and reflected in my beauty.

Your Turn

What part of yourself do you find the most beautiful? Your eyes, your hair, or your strong legs might be the first things that come to mind. But don't forget about the characteristics that make you beautiful on the inside. Are you a joy spreader? Do you pray for your friends? Are you compassionate and kind? Do you help people in need? Do you make a point to give others encouragement and compliments? Write down these qualities, too! This exemplifies your true beauty! (If you need more ideas, read through 1 Corinthians 13 and Galatians 5.)

My best beauty qualities:

_____

_____

_____

_____

_____

_____

_____

_____

_____

CHAPTER 2

Congratulations! You Made Dust Today
Eating Well

The other day I dusted the library at Whit's End. Sometimes I love my job. Other times I'm dusting.

I groaned in frustration. "Why is there so much dust?"

Just then Eugene came in. "An excellent inquiry, Miss Kendall," he said. "A simple scientific answer can explain the quantity of dust on God's creation."

Ah, Eugene . . . he always knows what I need to hear.

"Um . . . what?" I asked.

"Surely you are aware that what we call *dust* is primarily human skin cells that have been naturally shed."

"Ewwww, gross!" I said, dropping my dust cloth. (Or should I say skin-cell cloth?)

"To the contrary," Eugene asserted. "I find it fascinating. Were you aware that the outer layer of your skin regrows every single month? The human body produces more than twenty-three million new cells each *second*.[1] Every fourteen seconds, your body produces *more* cells than there are people in the United States!"[2]

I looked down at my arms and legs. Just a minute ago, I would have thought they were so . . . arm-y and leg-y. Now I looked at them like flailing, skin-flaking machines. "Wow, I'm pretty amazing."

"We are wonderfully made." Eugene nodded. "If you want, when you're done dusting off these books, we can—to borrow the colloquialism—'dust off' a few books together."

"I'd like that, Eugene," I said.

After I finished my shift, Eugene pointed out a couple of books that had some amazing facts on how God created us. Like . . .

- With sixty thousand miles of blood vessels inside the average human body,[3] you could wrap all of your arteries, capillaries, and veins around the earth two and a half times.

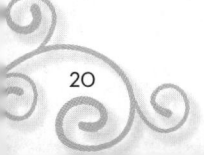

- Your belly button houses thousands of bacteria. It's like a rain forest of beautiful bacteria.[4]
- Our muscles are even more powerful than we think. Our strength is limited to protect our tendons and muscles from harm. But this limitation can be overcome during an adrenaline rush. People have lifted boulders or even cars off people they love who were injured or in danger![5]
- Humans produce different tears depending on the reason they're crying. When put under the microscope, tears from grief, hope, or peeling onions are all chemically different from each other.[6]
- Not only are your fingerprints and toe prints completely unique, but so is your tongue print. (But I don't recommend doing an ink smudge with your tongue.)[7]
- We blink every few seconds, without even thinking about it. This blinking keeps our eyes clean and moist. If we didn't automatically blink, our eyes would dry out within minutes and possibly be damaged.[8]

God's Crowning Creation

Isn't it amazing that God thought through all these details when He created us? Your body is far more advanced than any computer or robot. It allows you to sing and swing, yell and yodel, dream and problem-solve, smell and taste. Your body can heal itself, grow hair and fingernails, and be trained to run for miles. Have you ever thought about how your muscles, bones, brain, and eyes must all work together for you to traipse down the stairs, ride a bike, type an e-mail, or run cold water over your hand after you accidentally burn it on a hot stove? (Not like I'd ever be that absentminded.)

It's obvious that the human body is pretty amazing. But we can quickly become critical of our *specific* bodies. We sometimes focus on what our bodies are not—not fast enough, pretty enough, thin enough, developed enough—so we don't appreciate how incredibly astounding they *are*.

We wish we could change this or that about ourselves. I hear it all the time from the girls at Whit's End, from people trying on clothes at department stores, and even from my own lips. Instead of thanking God for our awesome bodies, we focus on what we consider wrong with them.

When you think about it, it's sort of like a toy complaining to the toymaker that he made a mistake. Or like a piece of clay arguing with the potter, like it says in Isaiah 45:9 (NLT):

> *Does a clay pot argue with its maker?*
> *Does the clay dispute with the one who shapes it, saying,*
>   *"Stop, you're doing it wrong!"*
> *Does the pot exclaim,*
>   *"How clumsy can you be?"*

Who knows better, the potter or the clay? The toy or the toy-maker? Yet how often do we complain about how God created us? How often do we tell our Creator, "You did it wrong!"?

Think about it from God's perspective. How does He react when we grimace at the bodies we see in the mirror? Maybe it's something like this:

You: Ugh . . . my nose is so big.

God: What?! I love that part of you. Did you know your sense of smell is completely unique, just like your fingerprints?

You: And my knees are really bony.

God: I gave you those legs because you're going to run cross-country and take your team to the state championship. You'll see.

You: I wish my eyes were blue instead of brown.

God: I designed those eyes. I think they're beautiful, and so will your future husband.

You: But why can't I be a little smarter? I'm having such a hard time in biology.

God: I gave you an imaginative brain to think outside the pages of a textbook. Right now you're learning perseverance and dedication. In a few years, you'll see how dedication and creativity will lead to amazing opportunities. Your difficulty isn't that I forgot about you, but that you forget I have so much planned for you.

You: I don't like who I am, God. You really messed up.

God: If only you could see yourself as I do. I designed you with care and intent. I love you—and every inch of you was designed out of that love.

Seeing ourselves through God's eyes isn't easy, especially with the image-focused society we live in. But instead of wondering how the rest of the world looks at us, we need to rest in the truth that He made us miraculously and beautifully. Just look at what David wrote in Psalm 139:14: "I praise you because I am fearfully and wonderfully made; your works are wonderful, I know that full well."

What if we could say that to God and really mean it?

I'm Too Fat

Sadly, so many girls struggle with wanting to be thin. The media doesn't help, since many models are extremely underweight. Our society tells us that thinner is better, even if that's dangerously thin. I searched the Internet and found that twenty years ago, "models weighed 8 percent less than the average American woman." These days, they weigh 23 percent less.[9] That's unhealthy. And that's what many of us are comparing ourselves to.

How can we not feel pudgy in comparison, even if we're at a perfectly healthy weight?

Morgan from Juneau, Alaska, has seen her friends try to meet an unrealistic objective. Check out the question she sent in:

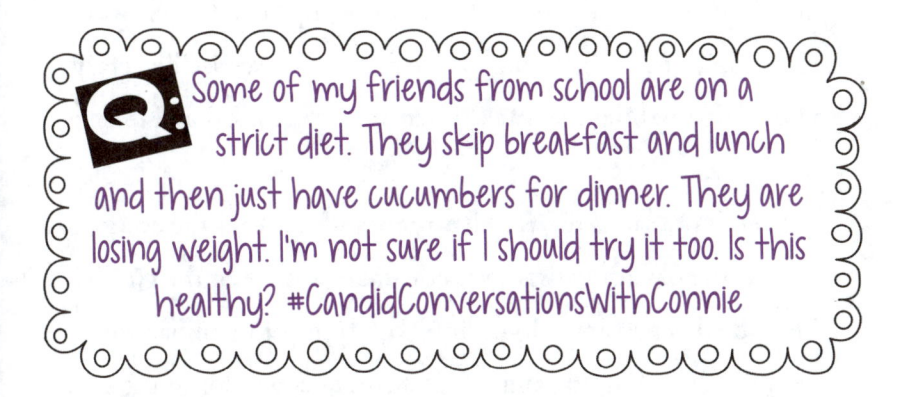

> **Q:** Some of my friends from school are on a strict diet. They skip breakfast and lunch and then just have cucumbers for dinner. They are losing weight. I'm not sure if I should try it too. Is this healthy? #CandidConversationsWithConnie

I can answer Morgan's question in three words: Nope. Nada. Not-at-all. (Okay, that last word was sort of three words.)

Growing bodies need nutrients . . . and cucumbers won't cut it. You need vitamins and minerals that come from a variety of foods. Avoiding a well-rounded diet can stunt your growth and development, diminish your brain's ability to work, decrease your energy, and even permanently damage your organs.

When girls (and boys in some cases) become so obsessed with being skinny, they are at risk of developing an eating disorder. It sounds like Morgan's friends might be heading in this direction—and that's dangerous.

Morgan should talk to her parents so they can let the other girls' families know what's going on before these girls develop bulimia or anorexia nervosa (or anorexia for short).

When I lived in California, and even when I came to Odyssey, I knew girls who put their looks above their health. Some of these girls would eat lots of food and then throw up later. Others would eat tiny amounts—like Morgan's friends—and exercise like crazy to burn off anything they ate. Either way, it was a sad and lonely way to live.

Even more sad is the fact that thousands of teens die every year because of eating disorders. Fortunately, none of the girls I knew died. They got help in time. But some of them had to spend time in a hospital and see a Christian counselor to get healthy.

Not that I'm trying to scare you, but the dangers of eating disorders can haunt you for the rest of your life. Here are just a few of the side effects:

- Very slow heart rate and low blood pressure (This increases the risk of heart failure.)
- Loss of bone density (If you lose bone strength while you're young, you'll have weak bones your whole life.)
- Muscle loss and weakness
- Fainting and constant tiredness
- Hair loss
- Dry, discolored skin
- Tooth decay
- Liver damage[10]

If you see a friend becoming dangerously skinny, do something about it. Confronting her about her weight loss likely won't help, because one of the symptoms of an eating disorder is that a girl never believes she's skinny enough. Even when everyone around her thinks she looks like a skeleton, she continues to lose weight. To her, it feels like she's in control of her life. To everyone around her, it's obvious she's out of control. That's what happened with Penny's friend Paisley.

Penny's Story

Paisley came to school at the beginning of my seventh-grade year. She was funny, smart, and creative, and she loved Jesus. I never thought of her as heavy, but she always seemed concerned about her weight. She'd flip through magazines and point out pictures, saying, "I wish I looked like this."

Pretty soon I noticed she was constantly on some diet. The celery and orange diet. The grapefruit and asparagus diet. I tried to convince her to try the french fry and milkshake diet—but it never worked. She was really proud of herself for having the willpower to skip a meal or eat only celery. So I watched Paisley grow skinnier and skinnier.

But as her body grew smaller, her temper grew bigger. She'd go off on me if I even mentioned she was too thin. She accused me of being "jealous" or wanting her "to be fat and miserable." Eventually she stopped hanging out with me. I noticed that her face became more gaunt and skeletal. The beautiful auburn hair she once wore in a thick ponytail looked thin and lifeless. After a few months of arguing with her parents and falling into a deep depression, Paisley was hospitalized.

I saw Paisley again after a long recovery. She looked a little healthier but said she still struggled every day with eating. She said she looked back at photos of herself in eighth grade and couldn't believe she looked that awful.

"Penny, I looked like I was almost dead! But the weird thing is, I'd look in the mirror and only see the fat. It was so messed up."

Listen up, girls. If you think you might be developing an eating disorder, please let someone know. Your mom, a counselor at school, a youth leader, or some other trusted adult. You may feel like it's something you can get over on your own, but you need to allow people you love to support you through it.

And if you're concerned about a friend who rarely eats or who throws up in the bathroom after lunch, be a true friend and let an adult know what's going on. You could save your friend's life.

Here's a Secret...

As you grow up, you'll go through awkward phases. The greasy-hair phase. The zits-covering-half-your-face phase. And the gaining-weight-before-your-height-catches-up-with-it phase. (We *all* go through that last one.)

As our bodies prepare for a growth spurt, we become really hungry. It feels like we always need more food. We start getting seconds or thirds at dinner (even when it's meat loaf). One bowl of cereal becomes three, and . . . wait, *did I eat all those pretzels*? The result? We start gaining weight, and we notice it.

In many cases, all of that extra weight is about to be *stretched* out as we grow four inches and two shoe sizes in a matter of months.

Don't be surprised if you go through times of feeling like you have too much baby fat, or your legs are out of proportion with the rest of your body, or you're too lanky. That can all happen in the same semester! You can't predict what your body will do. Just try to remember that what you see in the mirror will likely be temporary. If you continue to eat healthy foods, your height, weight, and proportions will all even out. Be patient—and don't take extreme measures.

Also, girls tend to have growth spurts earlier than boys. I thought I might be a basketball player in sixth grade because I was taller and weighed more than the boys in my class. If you feel that way too, it's perfectly normal. I finally stopped growing (and never developed the coordination to be a basketball star). And all the boys eventually passed me up. When the time is right, their bodies will go through changes too.

Choose Helium over Wooton Air

We hosted a birthday party at Whit's End last week. I was running behind (again), so Wooton volunteered to help me decorate. As he put the finishing touches on a colorful display of streamers, I looked down at my watch.

"Oh no! I'm late picking up the monkeys!"

"That's okay," Wooton told me. "They're not known for being punctual. Orangutans, on the other hand, would be annoyed."

"No, not real monkeys," I said. "Hand puppets."

"Oh, then I'm sure they wouldn't mind you being late," Wooton said. "Puppets are really good at just hanging around."

"But I told the party store I'd pick them up by now. We're doing this puppet show, since Micah loves monkeys and—oh, never mind! I need to run. Can you please fill up all these balloons while I'm gone?"

I gestured toward a box of balloons.

"No problem. Just call me the Balloon Baboon. Get it? Because we're talking about primates and—"

"Yes, Wooton. I get it," I said, rushing out the door. "Thanks!"

When I returned half an hour later with armloads of smiling monkeys, I looked at the ceiling. Zero balloons. *What was Wooton doing this whole time?* I wondered. Then I noticed balloons all over the floor. Wooton was leaning against the wall, red-faced and breathing heavily.

"Did you blow all these up?" I asked.

"Yes . . . and . . . I'm so out of breath. I think I need some oxygen."

"Didn't you notice the helium tank?" I pointed to the metal

canister that stood right next to the box of balloons. I thought for sure he knew about it.

He didn't.

I had wanted floating balloons for the party. Helium makes a balloon soar to the ceiling, because helium is lighter than air. But when we blow up balloons with our own breath, they fall down to the ground.

The food we eat is kind of like that. When we eat healthy foods—fruits, vegetables, meats, and grains—our bodies soar. We don't literally float into the air, of course, but our bodies look and work their best. On the other hand, filling our bodies with unhealthy foods—fries, sugary stuff, and hot dogs—makes our energy slump like a sad, breath-filled balloon. So even though we might feel full after eating four brownies or a bag of potato chips, we're filling ourselves with "Wooton air." Those foods aren't providing our bodies the nutrients they need to perform.

Eating Is Healthy

The key to being healthy isn't trying to fit into a certain mold of what you "should" look like. God gave you an *amazing* body, and He's entrusted it to you to take care of. Your body needs nutrients to function and grow, so make sure you're eating *real* food. Foods fried in oils, packed with preservatives, and stuffed with sugars aren't "real" foods. They're chemicals packaged to look like foods, but they don't carry the same nutrients that foods naturally have.

Everything you put in your mouth will make you either more healthy or less healthy. So try to center your meals around fruits, vegetables, salads, eggs, whole-grain breads, meats, and some dairy products. I attempted to grow a garden so I could get the freshest vegetables possible. Though my garden failed, I've tried to succeed in eating foods that look exactly how God made them.

At the same time, don't feel guilty if you enjoy a treat every once in a while. I'm around yummy stuff all the time at Whit's End. Sometimes I need to taste-test the latest ice-cream flavor to make sure it's good. (It always is.) But too much sugar will actually deplete your energy.

And don't forget how much sleep and exercise affect your energy level. Getting a lot of both is a good idea. To prove my point, I wrote out my schedule for two days last week. One day I started out making not-so-great choices. The other day I made better choices. Check out the difference.

Tuesday

1:00 a.m.—I stayed up late playing video games with Penny and Wooton. I crashed into bed and fell asleep immediately.

7:00 a.m.—The alarm went off way too early. I pressed snooze.

7:30 a.m.—I finally dragged myself out of bed. I was running late. I hurried and got dressed, forgot to brush my hair, and ran to the car.

9:00 a.m.—Since I didn't have time for breakfast, I gulped down a soda and ate a couple of donuts.

11:00 a.m.—Sugar crash. I drank another soda to keep up my fading energy. I didn't have time to pack my lunch, so I had a sundae instead.

2:00 p.m.—Eugene seemed especially annoying today. *Why should I care about his latest invention that I can't understand... or even pronounce?*

5:00 p.m.—I was blah all day long and couldn't wait to get home. I just wanted to sit in front of the TV. I grabbed some fast food on the way home.

As I sat slumped on the couch, feeling bloated and slug-like, Penny asked, "Wanna play Scrabble tonight?"

"Nah," I told her. "I think I'm going to turn in early."

Wednesday

10:00 p.m.—I crawled into bed. As I drifted off to sleep, I thought about my day and thanked God for my friends.

6:30 a.m.—I woke up before my alarm clock. I had time to pack a lunch, make some bacon and eggs, and walk to Whit's End. It was a beautiful, sunny day.

9:00 a.m.—It was busy, but I stayed up on my cleaning and enjoyed my talks with the customers.

11:00 a.m.—I was getting hungry, so I ate the turkey sandwich, salad, and pear I packed earlier. Perfect.

2:00 p.m.—I was super productive. I rearranged the Bible room, created some sets in the Little Theater, and went on an Imagination Station adventure with Olivia. I snacked on some carrots midafternoon.

5:00 p.m.—I decided to go rollerblading with a bunch of the girls. Then we went home and made tacos. I accidentally dropped mine and turned it into a taco salad. But it was still delicious. It was a fun day.

See how making a few smart decisions affected my whole day? Here are some of the healthy choices the girls and I shared:

TAMIKA: I try to do something active every day after school, even if I'm feeling worn out. Just fifteen minutes of jumping on the trampoline or going for a quick bike ride reenergizes me.

CAMILLA: I pack fresh, crunchy veggies in my lunch—and an apple for a snack, instead of a pudding cup.

OLIVIA: I stopped eating in front of the TV. It seemed like I could polish off half a carton of ice cream while I watched a show—just because I wasn't really paying attention to how much I was eating.

CONNIE: Cutting out foods that are bad for me wasn't easy. Sure, I felt better when I gave up nachos and soda, but I also felt, well, hungry! So I learned to replace unhealthy snacks with healthy ones—like fresh peaches, whole-wheat banana muffins, or chicken salad with celery sticks. I ate as many of these healthy treats as I wanted. And they were so delicious I didn't miss my nachos and soda . . . usually.

EMILY: When Grandma suggested chamomile tea before bed to help me sleep, I thought, *Gross! Who'd want tea a camel would eat?* But I learned I really like it. And it does seem to help me fall asleep. I always avoid sugar a few hours before bed too; otherwise I feel all wired up when I want to sleep.

PENNY: I'm usually not hungry in the morning, so I used to skip breakfast. Connie told me that eating breakfast is what gives me energy for the rest of the day. So I started grabbing chocolate-chip cookies to eat. Then she told me that I should try to have a healthy breakfast. Now that I'm eating oatmeal or yogurt in the morning, I really do notice a difference.

Your Turn

Take a day to record what you eat. For this task, don't change your habits. Try not to count calories or eat as little as possible. Be honest and really examine how healthy you're eating. Jot down how you're feeling throughout the day too. It's easy to underestimate how many chips or servings of ice cream you consume. That one bite can easily become two bowls.

_____

_____

_____

_____

_____

_____

_____

_____

_____

Go back and see how you did. Are there any changes you should make? Don't focus on dieting or quick ways to lose weight. Just try to recognize when your snacks are less than healthy or if you're eating lots of sugar when you feel depressed; then you can make plans to adjust your habits.

Chapter 3

How to Avoid Being Attacked by a Toaster
bYOUtiful

"Aaack! Who are you?" Penny screamed. "Get out of my house!"

She frantically waved a toaster at me as I stepped in through the back door.

"Penny, it's me . . . Connie!" I told her, stepping backward to avoid the flailing cord.

She narrowed her eyes, examining me more closely. "It is you," she said, calming down. "Why do you look so different?"

I plopped down in a kitchen chair. "I went to the mall to buy a new sweater, and one of those cosmetic-counter girls convinced me to get a makeover. But what are you doing with that toaster?"

"Oh, the toaster was just the closest thing to wave around in a threatening manner," Penny said. "I figured I could at least defend myself by throwing burnt bread crumbs in an intruder's eyes."

"Good plan," I told her. "Or at least a better idea than my makeover."

"Yeah," Penny grimaced. "You kinda look like they covered you in papier-mâché and then painted it with glitter. You might even be flammable."

That wasn't quite the compliment I'd been hoping for. "I thought the makeover would be fun. Then Kimmy, the cosmetics lady, pointed out all my flaws and told me she could fix them."

"Wow, so what kind of mascara can get you to work on time?"

"You know what I mean—my facial flaws. She informed me I have a crooked nose, eyes that are too far apart, unruly eyebrows, and too-low cheekbones."

Penny rolled her eyes. "Kimmy sounds lovely."

"But now that's all fixed. Can't you tell? *Ta-dah!*"

Penny tilted her head. "I don't think *fixed* is the right word."

"I agree. I didn't want to be rude, so I let her cake all this makeup on me. I should've said something before she went too far."

"You look fine . . . but not as good as Connie."

"But I *am* Connie."

"Exactly. But the normal, nonflammable version of Connie is my personal favorite. Crooked nose and all."

"Thanks." I smiled. "I'm going to wash off this makeup. It's making my face itch."

"Let me know if you want to borrow my paint scraper," Penny offered. "Oh, and then do you want to get something to eat?" She looked at the toaster in her hands. "For some reason, I'm craving toast."

Your Unique Beauty

I guess I've always been a little insecure about how I look. In high school, different girls rose through the popularity ranks. Blonde, blue-eyed Mindy wore cute skirts and headbands every day. Natalie sported spiral-shaped, red curls, a chipper personality, and paired combat boots with pearls. Trixie had beautiful raven-black hair, starred in all the musicals, and was a champion pole-vaulter.

I tried to be like each of them. They seemed to have it all together. I thought if I could be more like them, my life would be better. In my mind, just regular Connie Kendall with the ponytailed, brown hair and blue sweater wasn't anything special.

Then one day my mom grabbed her camera.

"You want to come down to Trickle Lake with me?" she asked. "I'm going to take some pictures of the sunset."

"Sure," I agreed.

I'm glad I did. The sunset was beautiful. Orange and purple, with pink clouds that illuminated the sky. Mom snapped a few dozen photos and declared it "the most beautiful sunset ever."

The next afternoon I asked if she wanted to go back, since there were only reruns on TV. I thought she'd jump at the invite, but instead she shrugged.

"Eh . . . no, thanks," she said. "We already saw the most beautiful sunset. Today's won't be as good."

I raised my eyebrows. "Well, it won't look the same. But it will still be pretty."

"We already saw the best one," she insisted. "What's the point?"

I pulled out her photo album. "There's no such thing as a best sunset," I told her. "Look at these." I flipped through the pages. Golden-red, cloudy sunsets. Electric blue-and-pink, clear-sky sunsets. And everything in between. "They're all beautiful," I said. "They're just different."

Mom gave me a knowing look. "Would you even say they're all beautiful because they're different?"

I thought about that for a minute. If a sunset looked exactly the same every night, it would become boring. What would be the point of watching it if you'd already seen it several times before? The beauty was that every night displayed a different show.

I nodded. "You're trying to tell me something, aren't you?"

Mom chuckled. She ran her fingers through my recently-dyed red hair. (I was in my be-like-Natalie stage). "Aren't you glad God didn't make every sunset the same or create a flower He thought was the prettiest, so He simply made them all like that? And I'm glad He didn't make us all look the same. I think God made you unlike anyone else." She gave me a hug. "Don't forget the YOU in beautiful."

Hmmm . . . bYOUtiful.

My mom was right. What makes the world so beautiful is that we all look different. You were given a unique beauty that no one else on this earth has. Your skin tone, hair texture, and eye color might not match up with the stunning actress on the movie screen. And that's great. You weren't meant to look like that actress. You were designed to look like *you*.

If you chase what you think is beautiful, you miss what's bYOUtiful right here. The very unique, God-planned beauty that's inside you.

What's Your Style?

Being beautiful has less to do with following trends and more to do with being confident in how you look. We've talked about how beauty on the inside is more important than external beauty. But when we look our best, it's easier to feel our best.

Everyone has their own personal style—the things they wear that make them feel confident. For some it might be skinny jeans and boots. For others it might be sundresses and flowers in their hair. For someone else, it could be all those things together! Your style is whatever makes you feel pretty.

As you grow up, you'll find the style and colors that look best on you. The shades that bring out your eyes or accentuate your hair. Certain clothes will look better on you than others. Some things will simply feel more "you." Pay attention to these discoveries. Follow those instincts more than what girls at school wear or how the mannequins are dressed.

Trends don't look good on everyone. I learned that in the feather-earring-and-streaked-hair days. So wear what makes you comfortable.

Style Quiz

Take this quiz to find your unique style.

1. The shoes you love to put on in the morning are . . .
    A. leather boots.
    B. ballet flats.
    C. high heels.
    D. tennis shoes.

2. Your favorite piece of jewelry is . . .
   A. the homemade friendship bracelet from your best bud.
   B. a chain with a pretty cross hanging on it.
   C. a chunky, colorful necklace.
   D. jewelry gets in my way—I prefer none at all.

3. The woman in the Bible you'd most like to meet is . . .
   A. Esther, a beautiful queen who used her quick wits and favor with the king to save her people.
   B. Ruth, the kind Moabitess who met her future husband working in the fields.
   C. Deborah, a bold judge who took action to encourage God's people to follow Him.
   D. Mary, the faithful and strong mother of Jesus.

4. Your favorite colors are . . .
   A. whatever is bright and eye catching. You love unique prints.
   B. pale blues, pinks, and yellows.
   C. black, red, purple.
   D. brown, white, green.

5. You're known as being . . .

    A. full of energy and creative ideas.

    B. thoughtful and a good listener.

    C. loud and funny.

    D. everybody's friend.

6. The characteristic that draws you to other people is . . .

    A. a wide, bright smile.

    B. thoughtful eyes.

    C. a big dose of energy and enthusiasm.

    D. being strong and fit.

7. If you could choose one type of makeup to wear, it would be . . .

    A. a bright-colored mascara.

    B. a pale eye shadow.

    C. a rich, dark lipstick.

    D. just lip gloss. I like to keep it simple.

8. Your favorite thing to put in your hair is . . .

    A. a one-of-a-kind scarf you picked up at a thrift store.

    B. an ornate silver barrette.

    C. an eye-catching hat.

    D. a ponytail holder to keep your hair out of your eyes.

9. Your dream dress would be . . .

    A. something you designed and sewed yourself.

    B. a full and flowing ball gown.

    C. a cute dress with a bold print.

    D. *Argh*. I don't really like dresses. But if I wear one, it has to be comfortable.

Score

If you chose . . .

Mostly As: You're a creative. You like to put together unique pieces that accentuate your one-of-a-kind personality. You think outside the box and like having the look no one else does.

Mostly Bs: You're a romantic. You like soft, flowing fabrics and beautiful jewelry. Roses and old movies are a favorite, and everyone loves your sweet and cheerful personality.

Mostly Cs: You're bold. You make a statement with your style—and it usually ends with an exclamation point. You might be a little loud, but you like it that way. Your friends do too. People notice what you're wearing, and you like the attention.

Mostly Ds: You're a natural. *Athletic, casual,* and *relaxed* are words that describe you. You don't like fussing over clothes and makeup—you'd rather spend your time being active.

Now before you revamp your whole wardrobe, remember that these are tendencies. It doesn't mean you'll feel the same way every day and in every situation. Sometimes you might like the big-statement necklace to go with your all-natural jeans and T-shirt. My point is: *all of these are okay*. One style isn't better than the others. Olivia likes to pair her favorite lime-green dress with a funky fedora. Penny prefers to paint the frames of her glasses in various patterns to match her mood. I like tucking wildflowers behind my ear on a walk. Camilla goes with a simple beauty routine—sunscreen, lip balm, and a T-shirt.

While it's fun to develop a personal style, what's most important is one simple rule: wear what makes you feel good and honors God. The "in" style often may not be the "right" thing to wear. What's right is what makes you feel most like who God created you to be!

My Best Beauty Tricks

Usually it takes a few mistakes before we figure out what makes us look our best. So hopefully I can save you from some beauty blunders by sharing what other girls (and women) have already learned. I asked some of the ladies around Odyssey to share their favorite tips:

>   Olivia: Don't go overboard with makeup. You want it to accentuate your features, not cause people to notice the

makeup. A little blush, eye shadow, lip gloss, and mascara go a long way. Strive for the "pretty" look, not the "Whoa! She looks like a cosmetic counter exploded on her" look.

Emily: My mom told me to apply makeup in natural light, if possible. Even if your face looks fine under bright bathroom lights, makeup appears harsher and darker in outdoor light.

Katrina: You want to make your eyes "pop" with shadow. Matching blue eye shadow with blue eyes will wash out your eyes instead of making them more noticeable. Use a complementary color instead. Browns and plums bring out blue eyes. Rust accentuates green eyes. And pinks make brown-eyed girls look their best. I have gray eyes, and my favorite colors to wear are lilac or peach.

Camilla: I want people to notice my smile. So I take care of my teeth and gums by brushing twice a day and flossing at least once a day. My parents like this too, because I always get great checkups at the dentist.

Tamika: With my skin tone, I can go a little bolder in my colors. I've also learned that changing my nail color is a great pick-me-up. Magenta, lime green, and sparkly violet nail polish can get me noticed in the right way.

Eva Parker: Hair dryers, curling irons, and straighteners can all help your hair look amazing. But avoid using them on a daily basis. They dry out your hair, making it brittle and frizzy. Combat that by deep-conditioning your hair once a week and getting regular haircuts to get rid of dry ends.

Dr. Lilly Graham: A lot of teen girls have oily skin, so avoid adding to the problem with oil-based cosmetics. Choose oil-free products instead. Keep a pressed powder in your purse to blot away extra shine. For those annoying zits, dab on acne-fighting products that contain benzoyl peroxide or other pimple-fighting ingredients. Tea tree oil can help too.

Penny's Story

During my sophomore year in high school, I was selected to receive the Outstanding Artist Award. I wanted to look my best for the ceremony, so my friend Bekka suggested I get some sun on my cheeks.

I *was* pretty pale. That previous winter, I'd been waiting for the school bus, and a kid mistook me for a snowman. (You should have seen how big his eyes got when I bit down on the carrot he tried to squash in my face.) So I thought, *Yeah, a tan. That's a great idea.*

Bekka and I went into her backyard, put down some towels, and promptly fell asleep in the sun. I woke up with a burning face and Bekka looking at me with the same expression as the little boy with the carrot.

"Uh . . . Penny?" she said. "I think we might have stayed out a little too long."

My mouth felt all stiff, so I couldn't ask what she meant. But I figured it out when I looked in the mirror. I was a lobster! I accepted my art award that week by walking gingerly across the stage, with a face like a peeling radish.

So now my life motto is "Sunscreen. Sunscreen. Sunscreen." (Well, that and "Everything tastes better with jelly beans.") We're not chickens, so our skin isn't meant to be fried. And once your skin is damaged, there's nothing you can do to repair it. Bad haircuts grow back, bad makeovers can be washed off, but bad decisions about not protecting our skin last a lifetime.

Even when it's wintertime or cloudy, smooth on some sunscreen. And don't forget to apply it twenty minutes before you go outside to give it time to soak in. Trust me, I'm now a sunscreen expert.

Thanks for all the good advice, everyone. Let me add this: Drink plenty of water. It helps cleanse your skin so you look healthier and brighter. Even your eyes will appear clearer and your lips fuller.

Here's a Secret...

The most beautiful people are those who are comfortable in their own skin. Really. Just look around you. They walk with confidence, smile easily, stand up straight, and are fun to be around. They like who they are—and that makes them attractive to others. So whatever "look" you like, be sure yours is bYOUtiful.

Your Turn

Dig through your closet and find some of your favorite clothes. Think about why you like them. Is it the color or fit? What are the things you get complimented on? Hold up certain colors and decide which ones look best with your complexion. (Sometimes it helps to have a friend or your mom give input.) Jot down some notes on the best colors and styles on the next page:

_____

_____

_____

_____

_____

_____

_____

_____

Now keep these ideas in mind the next time you go shopping. You'll end up with clothes and accessories you'll actually enjoy wearing!

CHAPTER 4

Lesson from a Thirty-Four-Pound, Pink Rhinoceros

Careful What You Buy Into

"I need Pinky Winky, Mom! I need Pinky Winky!"

A very obnoxious three-year-old with scraggly hair screamed those words a few hundred times on the video. How *incredibly* annoying.

Okay, fine. The three-year-old was me. My mom told me she recorded it so someday when I was older, I would have to watch it and be as annoyed as she was.

The only thing more annoying than that video was Pinky

Winky himself: a giant, pink rhinoceros that would light up and laugh when you squeezed his left foot.

I'd watched the commercial over and over as a toddler. "Light up!" "Laugh!" the smiling kids on TV squealed, clearly delighted with the massive, peppermint-colored pachyderm. "Mom, come in here!" I'd yell. "Hurry! It's Pinky Winky!"

I wanted to be just like the pretty girls on TV, with their big hair bows and colorful dresses. They laughed. Their parents laughed. Pinky Winky laughed. Clearly, Pinky Winky made life perfect.

On my birthday that year, I woke up to see Pinky Winky staring at me. A fat ribbon was tied around his neck. I screamed. He looked scary up close. I pushed him away. He fell off my bed and started to laugh. I laughed too. Pinky Winky was going to be great!

I carried him around all day. I asked my mom to squeeze his foot. She did, and Pinky Winky lit up and laughed. My dad squeezed Pinky Winky's foot and smiled. My grandma refused to get anywhere near Pinky Winky. (She always was a smart lady.)

The next day Pinky Winky stayed on my bed. After squeezing his foot so many times that I developed hand cramps, I didn't know what else to do with him. Somehow Pinky Winky wasn't as entertaining as he looked on TV. He stayed on my bed for a week, in my room for a couple of months, and tucked in a box in the basement for a year. He finally ended up in a garage sale.

Buyer Beware

You'd think I'd learn that things in advertisements aren't as great as they appear. Unfortunately, I can't say I instantly grew wise after growing bored with Pinky Winky. As a teen, I'd see an ad for "teeth-transforming toothpaste" or "the world's best-smelling deodorant" or "life-changing hair color" or "all-the-popular-girls-wear-them jeans," and I'd think, *I need that!*

The beautiful models smiling and laughing with their friends (not to mention getting looks from cute guys) convinced me that my life would be better if I used overpriced toothpaste . . . or wore expensive jeans.

I'm not a total idiot. I knew a new deodorant wouldn't transport me to an oceanfront pool party with a firepit and live music. But there was something about watching people have fun that made me want that life—and the *product* attached to that life.

Did you know advertisers don't sell products? They sell feelings. It's a well-known tactic in advertising. (I took a marketing class in college last year that explained everything.)

Think about this. Most beer is drunk by overweight men slumped on a couch. But how many commercials have you seen with a pot-bellied, middle-aged man drinking beer and watching football? None, of course. You see a party with attractive people being active and having a fantastic time.

Advertisers aren't paid to tell the truth about their products. Their success comes when they prey on our deepest hopes. The hopes that we can be successful, beautiful, popular, wealthy, and athletic. Something more than who we are now.

But here's the truth: regardless of what the ads say,

- You won't get a boyfriend because of a zit cream.
- You won't find the perfect life because of a perfume named after an actress.
- You won't win homecoming queen because of a toe-fungus medication.

Believe me. I've tried them all. (And I didn't even *have* toe fungus.) Everything we hope for can only be found in God, but I'll talk more about that later. For now, Penny wants to tell you a story about an ad she fell for.

Penny's Story

I saw an online ad for an avocado, vitamin E, and shea-butter facial mask that promised to make my skin look flawless. Naturally it was all-natural. I ordered it right away. After slathering some stinky, gloppy, green goop on my face, I let it sit for twenty minutes. Then I washed it off, just like the directions instructed. I looked in the mirror and . . . my skin looked the same. *But maybe it'll look different to other people,* I thought. So I found Wooton and asked him, "Do you notice anything different about me?"

He looked at me carefully. "You got your braces off!"

"Wooton! I never wore braces."

He peered closer. "Um . . . new haircut?"

"Nope."

Suddenly his eyes lit up. "Oh, I know! New perfume. You smell like a Moroccan beet salad."

Wrong again. I could have gotten mad, but instead we both decided we were suddenly hungry for salad and went to make one.

I kept trying the facial mask, but it pretty much never made a difference. (Except I did eat more salad. I guess it was the avocado.) A few months later, I found the perfect use for this "miracle" mask, and it worked like a dream. I spread it all over my face and hid in Wooton's closet. Then, when he came into the room, I jumped out with my green monster face. Wooton screamed like a cat stuck in a dryer. And that made the facial mask worth every cent.

Here's a Secret...

Advertising is a science. Businesses spend a lot of time and money figuring out what makes people buy things. Here are a few secrets I learned from my marketing class:

- Certain music and smells cause people to buy more. In one study, an appliance store pumped in an apple-pie smell, and the sales of ovens and refrigerators went up 23 percent.[1]
- Stores intentionally put small, impulse-buy items in the checkout lines. As people wait to pay, they start thinking, *Hmm . . . that candy bar looks really good. Ooh, maybe I could use more gum.* We end up buying stuff just because it's there.[2]
- The most expensive products are placed at eye level, so you notice them first. Take a look sometime when you're picking up laundry detergent with your mom. The better deals are placed up high or near the floor.[3]
- Companies spend well over $170 billion a year in the United States for ads on TV, in magazines, and on digital devices (which is the fastest-growing market).[4] Procter & Gamble, a makeup and personal-care-products company, spends the most

at nearly $5 billion. Thirty-five other companies also spend more than $1 billion a year, including Verizon, L'Oréal, Disney, Johnson and Johnson, Apple, Anheuser-Busch (beer), and McDonald's.[5]

The Hunt for Hope

If you look under my bathroom sink, you'll find a graveyard of beauty products that didn't live up to their hype. I have boxes of lotions that promised flawless skin. There are bottles of hair conditioner that guaranteed my lifeless locks would look like a supermodel's. And don't forget the tubes of mascara that said my lashes would stretch to North Dakota.

Did they work? Uh . . . nope. At least not as well as they promised. And a lot of them came with a pretty high price tag.

Yet we're continually tricked into believing that beauty can come from inside a bottle or cardboard package. The ads stir up discontentment, making us feel like we're lacking. Even earlier today, I saw an ad for a new car and thought, *Wow . . . I could use a new car.*

But I'm not unhappy with my car. My car works just fine. I'd been driving it quite contentedly only minutes before seeing that ad. I hadn't even considered getting a new one until the ad sold me on the idea that something better is out there—and that thing might make me happier.

It's nothing new. This deceiving message goes as far back as Adam and Eve. Think about it. Eve had it all: friendship with God, a beautiful place to live, a handsome guy, awesome animals everywhere. She had everything she needed to be happy, content, and fulfilled.

Except . . . for the *one* thing she didn't have. The tree stood in the middle of the garden. God had told Adam that he could eat from any tree, except from the tree of the knowledge of good and evil. Eve knew it too. It was the one fruit she wasn't allowed to eat. The slimy serpent Satan slithered over to Eve and whispered, "You're missing out. You'll be wiser and happier if only you eat that fruit."

Eve fell for the trick. She reached for the fruit and took a bite. Did the fruit live up to what the devil said? No way! Instead of happiness, it brought shame. Satan gave a great infomercial with bogus promises, and we've been falling for the same lie ever since.

That lie is ingrained in each of us. Thousands of years later, we *still* want something more to fulfill us. It's not a piece of fruit anymore. It's the promise of popularity or prettiness. It's a new phone or a trendy pair of jeans. It's the admiration of girls or the attention of boys. If only we had that, then we'd be happy.

We think.

The truth is, no one has found real hope—that fulfillment and joy—outside of a relationship with God. But often we can't see it. Adam and Eve missed it, and it was in the garden all along. Something shiny gets flashed before our eyes, so we follow it instead of following Christ. We keep looking for satisfaction in the next clothing trend, the next commercial, the next possibility.

Although advertisers can't deliver the hope they promise, true hope is readily available. And you don't have to empty your piggy bank to get it. Real hope—the hope of a life bigger and better than the one you woke up to this morning—is found in a God who is bigger and better than anything a new sweater (or anything else) can offer.

Consider this verse. It's great inspiration: "'For I know the plans I have for you,' declares the LORD, 'plans to prosper you and not to harm you, plans to give you *hope* and a future,'" (Jeremiah 29:11, emphasis added).

Hope. Something better. God wants you to find joy and goodness. He promises amazing blessings . . . and His promises never fail. He knows you'll never find real happiness in a lip gloss or even in a thirty-four-pound, pink rhino. Your hope and joy can only be found in God. Sorry, Pinky Winky.

Read what He says in the next two verses of Jeremiah: "Then you will call upon me and come and pray to me, and I will listen to you. You will seek me and find me when you seek me with all your heart" (29:12-13). The Lord tells you *how* to find true hope! Call on Him. Pray to Him. Seek Him . . . with *all* of you.

In Him, you'll find your hope. Your identity. Your purpose. Your fulfillment. Now that's something worth screaming about.

Your Turn

Watch a couple of commercials with your friends or parents and talk about them. Notice what the advertisers are really selling you. What are they promising? Are they trying to tell you that owning a certain car will make you successful? Do they want you to believe that eating a certain hamburger will make guys look at you? Discuss some of the tactics advertisers use, and write them down so you'll more easily recognize them in the future.

_____

_____

_____

_____

_____

Now make a list of what you desire. It's not wrong to want something. Maybe it's a new bike or longer hair. Maybe it's to have more friends or to make the tennis team. As you list each item, write next to it whether it's a *want* or a *need*. Sometimes it's hard to tell the difference. Ask yourself if these are God-given desires or something that's been stirred up because of an ad you've seen on TV or in a magazine.

Once you decide on your greatest desires (you may want to ask your mom for her help), make a plan for how you could achieve them. Maybe you'll need to save your allowance or take really good care of your hair. Then go back over your whole list and say a prayer over it. Ask God to keep these things from becoming your hope in life. Tell Him that whether you get them or not, you'll always find your hope in Him.

1. _____

2. _____

3. _____

4. _____

5. _____

6. _____

Chapter 5

Lesson from a Marshmallow

Waiting for Better

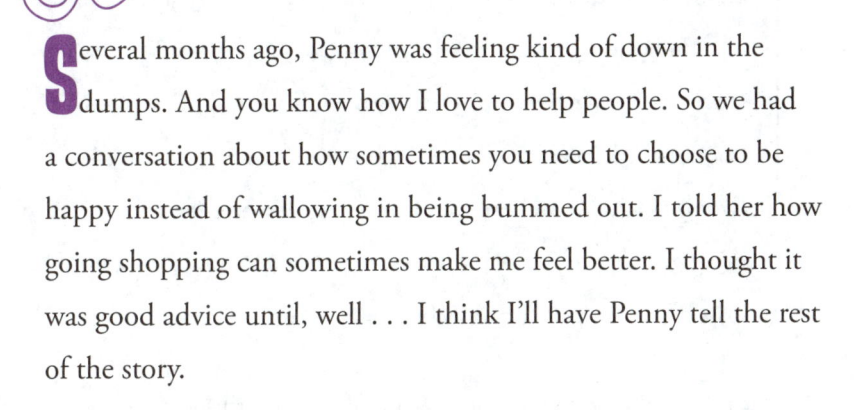

Several months ago, Penny was feeling kind of down in the dumps. And you know how I love to help people. So we had a conversation about how sometimes you need to choose to be happy instead of wallowing in being bummed out. I told her how going shopping can sometimes make me feel better. I thought it was good advice until, well . . . I think I'll have Penny tell the rest of the story.

Penny's Story

I went to the mall, determined to make myself happy. I'd heard that "retail therapy" could help cheer me up. As I walked through the mall entrance, the answer appeared written in the sky. Well, actually, it was a big banner hanging in front of the shoe store. It said, "Down in the dumps? Put on some heels and rise above it!" I took it as a sign—because it literally *was* a sign—that I should buy some new boots. They were expensive, but they looked really good on me. And you can't put a price on feeling good. Right?

I felt good for about twenty-seven minutes. Then it pretty much went downhill . . . all the way downhill. I tripped over my boots, rolled down a steep hill by the courthouse, and broke two ribs. Now when I see the boots in my closet, they do not bring me happiness. Instead, they remind me of an expensive lesson. I guess you can't buy happiness.*

---

* Want to hear more of Penny's story? Go to WhitsEnd.org and search for the Adventures in Odyssey radio drama "Happy Hunting," episode 720, album 56, *The Grand Design*.

Penny's story isn't uncommon. We live in an insta-world. Many of us have grown up getting what we want right away. Unhappy? Distract yourself with shopping or streaming an instant video. Hungry? Go to a drive-thru. Tired? Chug down one of those high-caffeine drinks. Want some information? Google it. Messages everywhere tell us "Buy now," "You deserve this!" and "Why wait?"

So we don't wait. We believe we should have everything we want right now. After all, what's wrong with that?

The Marshmallow Challenge

Eugene once told me about a study his college worked on. I put on my "I'm listening intently" face and prepared to daydream for the next three and a half minutes, but then he said it involved marshmallows. I immediately perked up.

So here's how it went. A bunch of five-year-olds were ushered into a room one at a time and sat at a table with a marshmallow in front of them. They were told they could eat the marshmallow now or wait while the researchers left the room. If they could hold out and not eat that fluffy, marshmallowy goodness, they would receive *two* marshmallows once the researchers returned. Eugene said half the kids ate their marshmallow before the researchers came back. Some gobbled it right away. The rest of the five-year-olds waited and received another marshmallow. I have to admit, if I'd been at that table, the first marshmallow would have disappeared like a rabbit down a hole. In fact, as soon as Eugene mentioned "marshmallow," I grabbed a bag from under the counter at Whit's End and munched on several as he told the story.

"Years later," Eugene continued, "the researchers contacted the subjects of the study to see if the lives of the children who waited for the marshmallow were any different from the lives of the those who ate the treat immediately. And you won't believe what they discovered."

"Bwup?" I said. (Because that's how *What?* sounds when your mouth is crammed with marshmallows.)

"The children who waited and received the second marshmallow performed significantly better on standardized tests as teenagers, had far fewer problems with drugs or obesity, and demonstrated they handled stress better than their peers."[1]

All that from a marshmallow. Wow!

The belief, Eugene explained, is that kids who are able to delay gratification (or wait for something that will make them happy) tend to work harder for their goals. In other words, they'll wait patiently in order to achieve better results.

The Bible calls it self-discipline. When you have self-discipline—the ability to put off your get-what-you-want-

and-get-it-now attitude—you tend to be healthier, earn better grades, excel in sports and extracurricular activities, and make wiser choices. In fact, having self-discipline is the only way to achieve what's really important in life. The apostle Paul put it this way to his young friend Timothy: "Discipline yourself for the purpose of godliness" (1 Timothy 4:7, NASB).

I asked the girls if they ever experienced the positive benefits of showing self-discipline. They had some great thoughts:

CAMILLA: Some people think I'm a natural athlete. I do have natural talents, but the real reason I'm so good at soccer is because I work really hard at it. Sure, sometimes I'd rather watch more TV, but that's not what's going to make me a better soccer player.

OLIVIA: I really wanted this super-cute coat I saw at Greenblatt's. I even had the money with me to buy it. But I'd planned on spending that money on Christmas gifts for my family. It was hard, but I decided to wait on the coat. The next week I got some extra babysitting jobs and asked Mom and Dad what additional chores I could do for money. Eventually I saved up the money for the coat. Then my mom showed me an ad in the newspaper. The same coat was on sale at a different store for half the price. Perfect! I'm so glad I waited.

Tamika: My friends invited me to go on a big shopping trip the day before a major test. I knew I needed to study, but it sounded a lot more fun to hang out with my friends. Finally I decided to stay home and study. The end result? My two friends got a C and D, and I ended up with an A-minus.

Emily: I got in the habit of surfing online right before I went to bed. Sometimes I would be online for an hour without even realizing it, so I ended up going to bed later. My mom had to drag me out of bed most mornings. Last night I made myself go straight to bed, even though I really wanted to text some friends. Today I felt better than I have in a long time. And best of all, Mom didn't need to dump ice cubes on me to wake me up!

God's Timing

Even though we live in an insta-world, we don't serve an insta-God. He's not a God where you insert three prayers and press a button, and out comes a can of happy life. Nope, learning to wait seems pretty important to Him.

Check it out for yourself. I've put some Bible stories in blog-post titles. See if you can match the title to the Bible character it refers to.

LESSON FROM A MARSHMALLOW

___ 1. How to Go 250 Miles in Only 40 Years

___ 2. Want a Baby? Try This 80-Year Fertility Plan

___ 3. Three Easy Steps to Rule the World: Get Thrown in a Pit, Be Sold into Slavery, Serve Jail Time

___ 4. Marry the Love of Your Life in Exchange for 14 Years of Hard Labor

___ 5. Do-It-Yourself Ark Building—Great Results in Only 120 Years

___ 6. Smell Fishy Insides for 3 Days—*Then* See God Work

A. Joseph (Genesis 37; 39)

B. Abramham and Sarah (Genesis 18:1-15; 21:1-7)

C. Noah (Genesis 6–7)

D. Jacob and Rachel (Genesis 29:1-30)

E. Jonah (Jonah 1–3)

F. Moses and the Israelites (Numbers 14)

Seems like God wasn't concerned about getting His followers exactly what they wanted as soon as they wanted it. (If you want to double-check your answers, here they are: 1. F; 2. B; 3. A; 4. D; 5. C; 6. E.) And I don't think that's changed in the last six thousand years.

As much as we want to use God like a drive-thru restaurant—make a prayer request at one window and pick up the answer at the next—that's not how He works. He thinks bigger than that. He even tells us in Romans 5:4-5 (NCV), "Patience produces character, and character produces hope. And this hope will never disappoint us, because God has poured out his love to fill our hearts."

God doesn't need to conduct a marshmallow study to know that delaying gratification is good for us.

Here's another question sent in from a listener. This is from Abigail in Park City, Utah.

> **Q:** My sister just got into college. They even gave her a credit card! She says it's great because now she can buy whatever she wants. But my parents warn her that it's not a great idea to use credit. I don't get it. A lot of people use credit cards—even kids my age. What's wrong with them? #CandidConversationsWithConnie

Back in olden days when people traveled by horse and an iPad was a thing that a pirate wore on his face, you had to work for something, and then you enjoyed it. That's how everybody lived.

You plowed a field, and you were able to eat.

You dug a well; you drank.

You built a fire; you had heat.

I'm not suggesting we go back a thousand years. I'm much better at vacuuming out my car than cleaning up after a horse. But today with payment plans, credit cards, and a surplus of anything we could ever want, we have this "Why wait when I want it now?" way of thinking.

Penny has a great story about this.

Penny's Story

I got my first credit card a few years back. At first I was super excited! To think I could buy whatever I wanted. Right away! Sure, I knew I'd have to eventually pay for it, but that all seemed like eons away. So I went shopping ... and then I shopped some more. I bought all kinds of stuff—most of which I didn't need—including some great yellow-and-pink-striped socks.

When I opened the bill the following month, I nearly fell off my new velvet, tiger-print beanbag chair. *Eek!* It was way higher than I expected. *No worries,* I thought. *I'll pay for it next month.* But then the credit-card company added all these fees called "interest," which didn't seem to be in *my* best interest at all.

I phoned the credit-card company to get an explanation. "I didn't buy any 'interest,'" I said. "And I'm plenty interesting, so can you please remove that charge?"

Well, I learned that's not what it meant. Those crazy fees were for not paying off everything I owed right away. Every month that I didn't pay the full balance, they charged more and more interest. So those four-dollar socks ended up costing me over ten dollars! And as great as they are, they aren't worth anything close to that.

It All Adds Up

I've had my own money-plus-not-thinking-ahead issues* but fortunately they didn't go as far as Penny's problem. Not that I figured everything out. The people who get credit for fixing my "credit" are Whit and my mom.

With their help, I learned that little expenses—a soda after school, some popcorn at the movies, a candy bar while waiting in

---

* To find out more about Connie's spending issues, visit WhitsEnd.org and listen to "A Little Credit, Please," episode 323, album 25, *Darkness Before Dawn.*

line at the store—add up. Once I came into work with a burger and fries from Quentin's Quick Burger, and Whit eyed me with surprise.

"I told you I'd have chili here for you," he said. "Did you forget?"

"No, I'll eat that, too. I just got hungry on the way here, and a burger sounded good. Then they asked if I wanted fries with it, and that sounded good too." I stuffed a few fries in my mouth. "It was only four bucks."

"Only four bucks," he repeated.

I shrugged. "Yeah, what's the big deal? I started earning an allowance at age twelve, so I've always had a little extra money to spend."

Whit pulled out a piece of paper and started writing down

Here's a Secret...

Practicing delayed gratification can make a big difference in all areas of your life. When we can put off dating, kissing, watching another show, or eating "just one more" cupcake, we're choosing something better for ourselves. Good things come to those who wait—especially those who wait on the Lord (Psalm 130:5).

numbers. "Let's pretend you put that four dollars into a savings account every day instead of spending it."

I decided to play along. "Okay . . ."

"Guess how much money you'd have in just over forty years."

"I don't know . . . a few thousand dollars or something."

He pushed the paper toward me. "Try over a million."

"What?" I looked closer at the paper. "I'd be a millionaire?"

"Yes, you would," he said. "When you factor in 10 percent interest, your money grows a lot over time."

Hmmm, I thought, *a million dollars just for giving up a burger and fries I don't really need.* Whit's example made me realize how I could reap huge benefits in the future if I made wise decisions with my money today. You just have to wait for it.

Just like Eugene's marshmallow study, by saying "not yet" to something that sounds good right now, we can say "yes" to something even better later.

Your Turn

Read the following verses. Circle what God promises to those who wait on Him.

> The LORD is good to those who wait for him,
> to the soul who seeks him. (Lamentations 3:25, ESV)

They who wait for the Lord shall renew their strength;
    they shall mount up with wings like eagles;
they shall run and not be weary;
    they shall walk and not faint. (Isaiah 40:31, ESV)

We do not want you to become lazy, but to imitate those who through faith and patience inherit what has been promised. When God made his promise to Abraham, since there was no one greater for him to swear by, he swore by himself, saying, "I will surely bless you and give you many descendants." And so after waiting patiently, Abraham received what was promised. (Hebrews 6:12-15)

Brainstorm some ways you can practice delayed gratification right now. Is it hard for you to be patient? Write down some things you can wait for instead of having them immediately.

_____

_____

_____

Chapter 6

The Gift of Toothpaste

Great Attitude=Gratitude

The pink dress made me look like a bag of cotton candy.

The black-and-white-striped dress made me look like I'd just escaped from prison.

The orange-fringed dress was okay . . . if I wanted to look like a pumpkin that lost a fight with a paper shredder.

Then there was the green dress. I knew as soon as I twirled in front of the dressing-room mirror that this dress was perfect.

"You look really beautiful, Connie." Mom smiled and then

glanced at the price tag. "Uh-oh. It's way more expensive than all the others."

I told her I'd do extra chores and contribute the allowance money I'd saved up (all sixty-seven cents). If that wasn't enough, I would get a job as a banana peeler for the monkeys at the zoo. Anything. I really, really wanted this dress.

Mom sighed. "You don't need to do any of those things. I've been saving up for something special for you. This can be it if you like it."

"Oh! IloveitIloveitIloveit!" I squealed. "Thank you, Mom!"

I went home and called my friends. They'd all bought their dresses for the high school dance too. We agreed to meet at my house and try on our dresses for each other. I couldn't wait!

The fashion show was so much fun. Then Emma came out in her dress—silky fabric in luminescent blue, iridescent layers draped perfectly. She said a well-known designer created it. Her dress cost ten times what mine did. Everyone oohed and aahed over it. I looked down at my dress, which had seemed so perfect. Suddenly I felt kind of miserable.

Have you ever experienced a happiness drop like that? One moment it feels like you're queen of the world—and the next, you're merely a grimy peasant.

Growing up, it was easy for me to start feeling bad for myself, especially when it seemed like someone had more than I did. And it wasn't just Emma and her perfect dress. It was also my friend Megan, whose grandparents gave her a brand-new car when she turned sixteen. Or my friend Taylor, who always looked like she belonged in a magazine.

We've all probably dealt with envy in one way or another. Camilla told me she used to get bummed out when she compared herself with her friends. But after taking a trip with her family, she began to see things a little differently.

Camilla's Story

I've always compared myself to others. I had an okay bike, but my friend Katelyn had an amazing Rock 8000 ZXV mountain bike. With purple paint and twenty-four gears, it could pretty much fly. Our house was fine, but Katelyn lived in a mansion. She had a TV in her room and her own bathroom with a Jacuzzi tub! I share a bathroom with Olivia and Matthew. I admit that my soccer socks don't smell like flowers, but Matthew sometimes smells like sweaty football socks even *after* he showers.

Then my family went on a trip to Kenya with Compassion International. Talk about an eye-opening experience! Families with five kids all lived together in a one-room hut about the size of my bedroom. They slept on thin straw mats, without a mattress, pillow, indoor bathroom, or cupcake-shaped nightlight. Some of the kids we met shared a toothbrush with their brothers and sisters, which made my sharing a bathroom not seem so bad. They made their own toys out of wire and cardboard—things I'd throw in the trash.

But that wasn't the most surprising thing. Do you know what was? They were happy. What they had was enough. They'd run in the sun barefooted, kicking a ball with their friends and laughing. If they had food that day and their family was together and healthy, their faces beamed with smiles. They even tried to give *me* gifts. Talk about generosity!

When I landed back at the Odyssey airport, I had a new perspective. I had so much. After seeing those little one-room huts, our house seemed massive. We could probably fit a hundred of our Kenyan friends in it! And there was food everywhere I looked: the fridge, the pantry, the grocery store. It wasn't just rice and beans, but oranges, fresh veggies, and ice cream. To the kids in Kenya, peeling an orange would have felt like opening a present on Christmas morning. To us, it's just a regular morning.

For about a week, I remembered to be grateful for everything: hot showers, good schools, a family car, clean drinking water straight from the kitchen faucet. Even "luxuries" like straws, french fries, and birthday cake amazed me. Then I went to Katelyn's house. Once again the green-eyed monster reared its ugly head. *Why don't I have new, expensive jeans? Or her allowance? Or horseback-riding camp?*

My situation hadn't changed. (I still had the same great house, family, and friends.) But my attitude had. I didn't want to see only what I lacked. I was very, very blessed—beyond what I deserved—and I wanted to remember that.

I went home and posted pictures of my friends from Kenya all over my bulletin board. From my trip, I learned that more than one billion people in the world live on less than one dollar a day.[1] I'm so fortunate to have a family who loves me, a healthy body, a warm house, food to eat *every* day, shoes that fit, and a bazillion other things.

Figuring Out Happiness

We don't think of toothpaste, riding a bus to school, or fresh fruit as luxury items. But for much of the world, that's exactly what they are.

I found a statistic that said if your family has two cars, a home, several outfits in your closet, and money to participate in a hobby, then you are among the richest 5 percent of the people in this world.[2] That means you're more wealthy than 95 percent of the population! So does that make you happier than 95 percent of people too?

You'd think the math would look like this:

People with the most stuff = the happiest people

But if you gave that answer on a quiz, you'd be wrong. Often, people who have the most are the ones who complain the most. I know that was true of Emma, Megan, and Taylor. Camilla said that Katelyn was the same way. It's almost like the more we have, the more we want.

Instead of stuff making us happy, I've learned that this equation is true:

People who are the most grateful = the happiest people

Scientific studies show that people who show gratitude have higher self-esteem, experience better health, are less likely to suffer from depression, and feel happier overall.[3]

Happiness doesn't grow just because we have more things or

make more money. Those things actually have very little to do with happiness. People with less—but who are grateful for what they do have—are happier than people with more possessions and money, but who compare themselves to others.

Isn't that funny? It doesn't matter if you have the latest technology or the most expensive clothes. What matters is how much you appreciate the things you've been given. *That's* what creates joy!

Turn Grumbling into Gratitude

Ungrateful hearts aren't new to God. He's heard a lot of complaining. The Bible tells us that a few millennia ago, He rescued the Israelites from enslavement in Egypt. As Moses led God's people to the Promised Land, they grumbled . . . a lot. During a Bible study the girls and I went through, we saw how often the Israelites complained during their forty-year journey through the desert.

Tamika piped up. "I don't get it. The Israelites had seen miracles. The ten plagues. The Red Sea. Bread falling from heaven. The Ten Commandments. Water out of a rock! They weren't stuck in captivity. How could they complain so much?"

"You don't think you'd complain about wandering in the desert?" I asked her.

"Of course not! They were so much better off than they'd been before. I'd be doing cartwheels!"

The other girls nodded in agreement.

"But aren't we *just like* the Israelites?" I said. "God's given us salvation and grace, and Jesus. We have houses full of food—way more of a variety than the Israelites had—but I'm guessing some of you still complained about dinner last night."

The girls looked around at each other as I thought about all the times I'd complained that day.

"Well, it *was* cauliflower soup," Olivia spoke up.

All the girls laughed. But we got the point.

And the point is, *we* complain to God too. Just like the Israelites, we've seen God provide for us in amazing ways, and we always want more.

So the girls and I came up with a plan. First, we thought about the things that cause us to complain out loud or mutter silently to ourselves. After sharing about what gets us grumbling, we brainstormed ideas on how to live a life of greater gratitude. Here are some of our confessions and the ideas we had to grow more grateful:

OLIVIA: I have one of those friends . . . the kind who is good at everything. She's pretty, smart, talented, and athletic. Standing next to her, I feel like a blob of oatmeal—bland and pointless. I secretly wished I could be more like her. I always felt lacking.

With the girls . . . we talked about how God made me pretty amazing just like I am. When I'm busy being jealous of someone else, I miss out on what I've been given. On my bathroom mirror, I wrote down a list of talents and gifts God's given me: pretty hair, acting ability, lots of friends, a good brain for math. It helps to be thankful for what I have—instead of being stuck in the comparison trap.

TAMIKA: I realize that I often see the worst in things. Like when I went to the movies with my friends the other night, I complained to my mom that I couldn't go to the movie everybody wanted to see because she thought it was too violent. Then I complained that the popcorn was too salty. Next I whined to my friends that they picked terrible seats. Afterward I grumbled about how I didn't get to stay out as late as my friends did. I didn't even realize how negative I was becoming, until I looked back at my attitude. *Whoops.*

With the girls . . . we looked at the verse in Psalm 45:7 (NCV), "You love right and hate evil, so God has chosen you from among your friends; he has set you apart with much joy." I do want to love what is right and be set apart with joy. So I started to think before I spoke, asking myself, *What's the right way to act?* Rather than whine about the movie I shouldn't see anyway, I want to say "Thanks, Mom, for caring about what I watch and driving me to the movie." And instead of rolling my eyes at my friends' seat selection, I want to say, "Thanks, everyone, for hanging out with me tonight. I'm really glad I have friends like you."

PENNY: Some days it feels like Murphy's Law should be called Penny's Law, because everything that could go wrong *does* go wrong. I wake up late. The hair dryer gets stuck in my hair. I rip my favorite dress. And I can't find two matching shoes. By the time I get to class, I'm late and realize that I forgot my homework. So now I'm cranky and wearing one sneaker and one bunny slipper. It's 9:00 a.m., and the whole day is already ruined.

With the girls . . . we talked about the need to take a breath and notice the good things around us. No matter how disappointing a day is, we can always find a bright spot. Every time I want to complain, the girls encouraged me to think of three things to be happy about. So today I appreciated the beauty of a clear, blue sky; the gallon of maple syrup that Wooton gave me; and the smell of bacon. (I love bacon.) I soon realized happiness was all around. I didn't need to go out and *find* it as much as I needed to be still and *recognize* it.

With Thanksgiving . . .

God wants us to ask for things. He loves to hear our needs and wants. Philippians 4:6 (2011) tells us, "In every situation, by prayer and petition, with thanksgiving, present your requests to God."

Here's a Secret...

I spent a lot of time during my teen years complaining to my mom. My allowance wasn't big enough. She didn't get the cereal I wanted. I had too many chores. Blah, blah, blah.

Sadly my mom died not long ago. It felt like I'd been kicked in the stomach. When I look back, the things I complained about seemed pretty pointless. I regretted the time I wasted complaining. The moments I treasured were laughing with Mom when she tried to teach me to ice-skate (and both of us falling down more than we stood up). Or the times we made cookie dough before watching a movie together, or took walks along Trickle Lake in the fall and talked about anything and everything.

Since she passed away, I have a different perspective. These moments in life don't last forever—so we need to appreciate the times we have with our families, pets, and friends. Instead of seeing what's lacking, let's open our eyes to the many gifts we've been given.

Living a life of gratitude is simply living a life with a great attitude. It's noticing the good over the not-so-good, remembering to appreciate those around us, and stopping to give God thanks for the blessings He gives us every day.

Did you catch that little phrase in there? Go back and reread Philippians 4:6. Got it now? *With thanksgiving.* You might want to circle that phrase.

God enjoys blessing us, but He doesn't want us to behave like spoiled brats. He wants us to acknowledge the many gifts we already have. God doesn't want us to just ask for things; He wants us to thank Him for what is right in front of our faces.

Remember when Jesus healed the ten lepers of their disease? (If you don't, you can read about it in Luke 17:11-19.) Well, only one returned to say thanks!

"Where are the other nine?" Jesus asked. He'd given these men their lives back—yet 90 percent of them didn't even send a thank-you card.

A girl (I won't tell you her name) once came into Whit's End and asked if I would help her audition for a community theater program. I agreed. Then I realized—after it was too late—how much work it would take. I ended up spending hours coaching her, videotaping her (so we could watch her rehearsals together and critique them), and talking with the director to get pointers for what he was looking for. Here's the good news: the girl actually got the part! And the not-so-good news: right after finding out, she called her friends to give them the good news but completely ignored me.

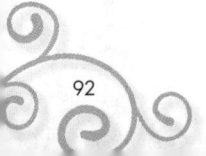

I have to admit it *really* irritated me. I'd put a lot of time into helping out Heather—I mean, the girl—and she didn't even say thank you. I didn't want a ticker-tape parade thrown in my honor (although that might have been nice). I just wanted her to acknowledge that I'd helped her succeed.

As I shuffled home, it occurred to me that I probably felt a little like Jesus did when He healed the ten lepers. I only helped Heather get a part in a play. He kept these guys from dying from a terrible disease. The least they could have done was say thank You. (Which was also the least Heather could have done.)

To be honest, most of the time I live like the nine lepers who didn't come back. Something good happens, and I'm already asking God for something else. I want to live like the one guy who returned, who knelt down in front of Jesus and said, "Thank You, thank You, thank You."

Your Turn

Think of fifty things you're thankful for. Moments of beauty or belonging. An event that made you smile. A time you felt close to God. A special friend. Your loving family.

The girls and I came up with these:
- A bird building a nest
- A kind word from a friend
- A warm house on a snowy day

- A hug from my dad
- Curling up in a blanket to watch my favorite show
- Clouds in the shapes of ice-cream cones
- My favorite song on the radio
- The gift of sight
- Laughter

Take some time to think of your own list of blessings and write them below.

Thank You, God, for . . .

_____

_____

_____

_____

_____

_____

_____

_____

_____

_____

THE GIFT OF TOOTHPASTE

Chapter 7

Careful with Those Hedge Trimmers!
Being Smart Online

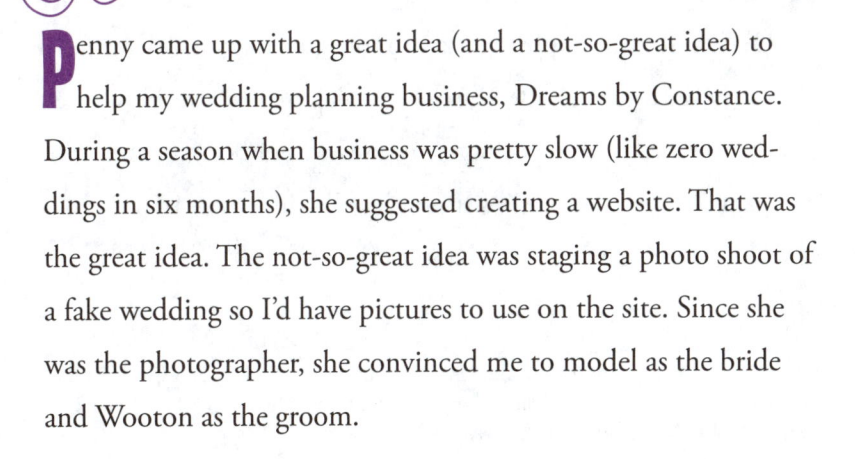

Penny came up with a great idea (and a not-so-great idea) to help my wedding planning business, Dreams by Constance. During a season when business was pretty slow (like zero weddings in six months), she suggested creating a website. That was the great idea. The not-so-great idea was staging a photo shoot of a fake wedding so I'd have pictures to use on the site. Since she was the photographer, she convinced me to model as the bride and Wooton as the groom.

Long story short, the photos got passed all over social media from people who believed the wedding was real. Talk about a debacle. We spent months cleaning up that mess . . . and returning all the wedding gifts from well-intentioned friends. (Not that I needed seven electric can openers and four doormats anyway.) My great-aunt in California planned a bridal shower. Wooton's family hired a private investigator to run a background check on me. My hairdresser stopped talking to me because I hadn't told her the news before the "wedding."*

I couldn't believe how quickly the news got around—even to people in different states and countries!

That's the power of social media. It's fantastic . . . *and* challenging.

Don't get me wrong. I love that I can Facebase with friends. So do the other girls in our little group, although they often go to Club Kidchat.

> OLIVIA: It's fun to post pictures of outfits I'm considering and have friends give feedback on which one is best. How awesome that I can get thirty responses in only a few minutes. I also post video clips from plays I'm in, so my friends who live far away can watch. So cool!

---

* Want to hear more about this wedding mix-up? Go to WhitsEnd.org and search for the Adventures in Odyssey radio drama "Something Old, Something New, Parts 1 and 2," episodes 713–714, album 55, *The Deep End*.

TAMIKA: I'm really happy that I can look up friends from the school I went to before I moved to Odyssey. I'm able to know what they're doing, so I don't miss them as much. When I see pictures of their birthdays or activities, it's like I can still be a part of their lives.

EMILY: If I'm looking for something to do, I just ask around online to see what everyone's up to. Pretty soon I have a bunch of different options. It's way quicker than texting every single person.

PENNY: Wooton posted some videos where he's making french toast while wearing a suit of armor. It cracks me up every single time.

CAMILLA: Sometimes I come across a verse or hear a quote from our youth pastor that I find inspiring. After I share it, I like hearing people's responses. I feel like I'm encouraging my friends.

KATRINA: I appreciate becoming friends with people of similar interests. I can participate in an online French literature book club—something that intrigues me, but which would be rather difficult to find in Odyssey.

For me, I love being able to share important moments in my life with a lot of people at the same time. And it's really encouraging to receive support from friends who live all over, even some from when I used to live in California. Whether I'm getting married or calling off a wedding, I can let everyone know at once. And they can offer congratulations . . . or sympathy.

Yep, social media can be a pretty useful technology. But there's another side of it too. Here's what the girls have to say about *that*:

> CAMILLA: Once a so-called friend got mad at me and posted lies all over Club Kidchat. She said I got caught shoplifting. Tons of people saw the post and believed her! She eventually apologized and took down her post, but months later, people still asked me about "that time you got caught shoplifting." Even when I told them it was a lie, I don't think they believed me.
>
> EMILY: I was once really mad at my brother, Barrett, so I posted this long, emotional tirade about how mean he was. I regretted it later, but by then a lot of people had seen it—including Barrett, my parents, and some friends. I ended up hurting people I really care about it. I wish I could take back those words, but I can't.
>
> PENNY: I got addicted to the "just one more" of social media. You know what I mean: *I'll just check out one more photo, click on one more link, share one more comment.* Without realizing it, I'd spend hours staring at a screen—instead of doing my homework, hanging out with my family, or finding my pet gerbil. My grades dropped, my family grew

irritated, and Jerry the Gerbil ended up chewing his way through a whole box of my favorite cereal.

TAMIKA: Some people started posting mean things about a girl at my school. It really got out of control. People bullied her. They called her fat and stupid and even worse things. She didn't come to school for a week. Even now, she hardly talks to anyone. I try to be her friend, but she doesn't trust anybody and just keeps to herself.

OLIVIA: Sometimes when my friends post pictures of themselves having fun, I wonder if my life is as exciting as theirs. I log off feeling not so great about my plain, boring, blah life.

KATRINA: Occasionally I find myself scanning information online when I should be doing something else. It becomes a mindless distraction that keeps me from doing more important tasks. The other day, Eugene wanted to go for a walk, but I was so busy reading blogs that I turned him down. It would have been a much better use of my time to go for a walk and be with my husband.

The Tragedy of the Shrubs

A while back, I noticed the shrubs in the backyard needed to be trimmed. I asked Mr. Parker if I could borrow his hedge trimmers.

"Um, are you sure you know how to use them?" he asked. "These are gas powered."

I'd seen people use them before around Whit's End. "Of course," I assured him. After all, how hard could it be?

It was a little more complicated than I expected. Those power tools are pretty . . . well, powerful. Thankfully, Mr. Parker had included the instruction manual.

"What are you doing?" Penny asked when she saw me poring over the manual on the porch.

"Learning how to not cut off all my fingers," I told her.

Penny looked at her hands. "Huh. And to think I've kept mine all these years without ever knowing I needed a book about it."

"Very funny," I said. "But really, this is dangerous." I pointed out some diagrams. "These safety features need to be set manually. And there's a right and a wrong way to hold the trimmers. You even need to stand the right way *while* you're holding them."

Penny shook her head. "Who knew keeping all your fingers could be so complicated?"

Social-media sites can be like hedge trimmers. They can be helpful tools that make life more beautiful. But if used carelessly, they can also be very dangerous. Know what the dangers are. Be careful with what you post, and know who you're sharing with. Become familiar with the safety features. It's also a good idea when you first start out to have someone you trust help you.

By the way, Mr. Parker is coming by on Saturday to give me a hand with what's left of the shrubs. (Huh . . . maybe "give me a hand" isn't the best term to use.)

The First Step

Some social-media sites require users to be at least thirteen. But it's on the honor system. So kids younger than that can sign up and lie about their ages (which is a very bad idea). Other sites don't specify. You might not be into social media yet—and that's great—but it's likely that someday you will. So now is the time to decide what kind of techno-girl you want to be.

Here are four common types of users:

1. *Consumed Callie.* Callie *loves* her computer. She's on it all the time. She spends hours playing games, surfing different websites, and watching videos. If she's doing research for a school project, she'll look up hours later only to realize she still hasn't started researching yet. She'll go to just about any site, thinking she's safe wherever her laptop takes her. Sometimes she ends up hiding her computer under her blankets at bedtime, just so she can spend a few more hours in a virtual world.

2. *Spill-It-All Sadie.* Sadie has tons of friends online—friends from school, friends from chat rooms, and friends from social media. She's constantly posting updates on Facebase. Since she's so friendly, she has no problem sharing information with others.

If they want to know where she goes to school, where she lives, or what she looks like—she's happy to share.

3. *Careless Cameron.* Cameron doesn't go online a whole lot. She's on a couple of social-media sites, but she doesn't think she's on them enough to mess with the privacy settings. And because she couldn't remember her password, she told all her friends so she could ask them what it is. She uses her computer to do research for school. But she'll use any search engine and go to whatever site pops up. She figures all the information is reliable if it's on the Internet.

4. *Wise Wendy.* Wendy thinks ahead when she's going to be online. She tells her parents and sets a timer so she doesn't waste her day. Her parents have decided thirty minutes is enough at one time, and she sticks to that. She uses sites that are approved by her parents, and her dad helped make sure all the privacy settings are in place. She limits the people she interacts with online to those she personally knows.

Can you find yourself in these four types of girls? Can you find some of your friends?

This is an important topic. The Internet constantly changes. New sites are developed, and new technologies take the place of what used to be cool. Even the social-media sites where you hang out now may be totally different in a couple of years. But the concerns and courtesies of being online will stay the same. Noelle from Rockwall, Texas, sent in a question that touched on this issue.

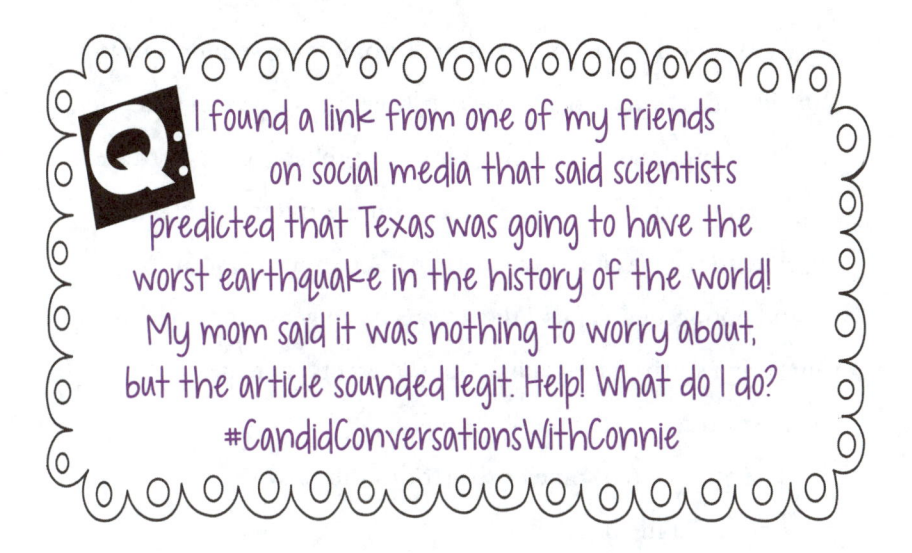

> **Q:** I found a link from one of my friends on social media that said scientists predicted that Texas was going to have the worst earthquake in the history of the world! My mom said it was nothing to worry about, but the article sounded legit. Help! What do I do?
> #CandidConversationsWithConnie

Well, Noelle, before you start sleeping in the bathtub with a trash can lid over your head, you might want to take another look at the source of the information. On the Internet, it's pretty easy for people to claim they're "experts," even if their only expertise is creating fake stories.

Here's an important rule to remember: Don't believe everything you see online. That goes for posts from friends sharing rumors about other people and official-looking sites that you might want to use for researching a school project. (Check with your teacher first to see if she thinks a website you're using is a reliable source.) Remember, even photos aren't necessarily proof of anything. Today, digital photographs can easily be altered to create the appearance of a ghost, a three-legged man, or even an earthquake in Texas.

Be skeptical when you're online. If something sounds unreasonable, illogical, or too good to be true, then be wary. Sites that offer you "free" products (except for shipping) probably can't be trusted. Act like my friend Emily when you're on the Internet and search for clues to see if a site lacks reliability. Look for the motives behind outrageous claims. And always try to get to the original source. If a story you're reading doesn't cite its sources, it most likely isn't true.

The girls shared some of the stories they saw this past week on just one social media site:

- Superstar actress loses 40 pounds by eating strange, exotic fruit.
- Huge tech company gives $1,000 to whoever shares this photo.
- If you love Jesus, share this picture of a cat jumping up and down on the couch. If you don't share it, something tragic will happen in your life!
- Try these simple tricks to get your hair to grow 9 inches in 30 days. Guaranteed!
- You just won $1,000,000! Call this number now!
- Just confirmed: State senator is actually an alien!

The Internet can be a great source for information. But because there are no fact-checkers to make sure everything we read is true, we need to use discernment. *Discernment* means "to wisely think something through," not just believe everything you hear. The apostle Paul wrote in Philippians 1:9-11,

> *This is my prayer: that your love may abound more and more in knowledge and depth of insight, so that you may be able to discern what is best and may be pure and blameless until the day of Christ, filled with the fruit of righteousness that comes through Jesus Christ.*

I want to pray that same prayer. By growing in the knowledge of God's Word and going deeper with our insights, we'll all be able to discern the truth. God gives us His Word, His Spirit, godly friends, and loving families to help us decide what's best. That goes for how we use the Internet, what we believe from social media, and how we act in every other area of our lives.

Here's a Secret...

Even my friends, who I think should know better, sometimes share rumors. (Penny just sent me a story on how brussels sprouts cause cancer. I'm pretty sure that's not true, and Penny just sent it because she hates brussels sprouts.) The stories can sound believable, so people share them without checking to make sure it's reliable information. Try your best not to pass along rumors; instead, ask a parent to help you find the original source and fact-check to see if a story you're reading is actually true.

When Not to Share

Just like people can make up "facts" online, they can also lie about who they are. "Friends" you meet electronically may not be who they claim to be. Anyone can go online, create a fake name, post a random photo, and pretend to be someone else. So that sweet twelve-year-old girl named Emily you met on a gaming site could actually be a forty-nine-year-old prisoner named Bruiser.

Again . . . don't believe everything you see or read online. And really, you shouldn't be communicating with anyone you don't know online unless your parents have given you a thumbs-up. Being smart includes not giving out information to people you don't know personally. I'm not saying this to make you afraid of the Internet, but you do need to be careful. Here's a lesson Olivia learned . . .

Olivia's Story

I started getting e-mails from a website that promised great free stuff with no strings attached. I thought, *Cool.* Although I never signed up to receive the e-mails, who wouldn't want free stuff? The e-mails asked for my birth date, my address, my phone number . . . and a bunch of other personal information. That's when I began to wonder, *Is this for real?* I showed the messages to my dad, and he told me to block the e-mails. It's *never* safe to share personal information with people over the Internet without a parent's permission. It's easy for criminals to come up with fake names, e-mail addresses, and profile pictures that look harmless. But they can use that information to steal your identity or do something even worse. I'm sure glad I talked with my dad.

Your Turn

Prayerfully ask God to help you have wisdom and discernment when you're on your computer or smartphone. Then consider your Internet habits. What are good reasons to be online? List some of the ways you've used the Internet in the past week. Think about what sites you went to and for what reason. Write down as many of the sites as you can remember. Then put a star next to each site that was worthwhile and a check mark next to each one that was a waste of time. After that, go back and circle the sites that were valid but you spent too much time on.

1. Good reasons to be online:

_____

_____

2. Sites I've visited this past week:

Chapter 8

When You're Just Like a Shaken Can of Coke
Think Before You Post

Ever play Two Truths and a Lie? Here are the rules: I tell you three stories about myself. Two of them actually happened. One is made up. You have to guess which one isn't true. Ready? Here are the stories:

Penny and I were walking through a department store, and we passed a mannequin holding the most ridiculous purse I'd ever seen. Covered in various prints and zippers, it seemed like the silliest thing in the world.

"Hey, look!" I said to Penny. "The purse company had a bunch of scraps left over and decided to sew them together and charge a bunch of money for it. They must count on part of the female population having no sense of style whatsoever. Right?"

I expected Penny to laugh. Instead, she looked embarrassed and was nodding toward a lady who was carrying the exact purse I was making fun of! Then it was my turn to turn red. *Oops.*

I was recording *Candid Conversations with Connie,* and Eugene kept correcting every single thing I said.

"The word is *conundrum,* Miss Kendall, not *conundumb.*"

"President Fillmore's first name was Millard, not Phil."

"Technically, curiosity couldn't kill a cat. Otherwise, there would be far more deceased felines."

During a commercial break, I grew so fed up that I had to tell him how I felt. "You think you know it all, don't you? Well, you're wrong about plenty of things!"

I went on for nearly a minute before I realized the commercials had ended and I was telling off a good friend on radios all across Odyssey. *Oops.*

I got cut off in traffic last Tuesday. Instead of complaining to my friends in the car about horrible drivers, I simply smiled and forgot about it.

Answers: True. True. How I wish it were true!

This might surprise you, but I sometimes blurt out things without thinking. Okay . . . if you've known me more than six and a half minutes, this doesn't surprise you at all.

As girls, we can get pretty emotional. We have hormones racing through our bodies, which can cause us to react strongly in a moment. (But the next day, that same thing may not seem like such a big deal.) That's normal and even healthy.

But what's *not* healthy is posting your emotions for the world to see. Your eight hundred closest friends do *not* need to know that your social-studies teacher is an ogre who has it out for you because she gave you a C on your last essay.

The girls shared an embarrassing Club Kidchat exchange they saw just this week:

CallieRae: You might think Madeline Green is nice enough, but she'll stab you in the back if you give her a chance. #DownWithMadeline

MadelineG: For anyone who believes anything Callie Morgan says, you're dumber than she is. She flunked her history test for a reason. #CallieLies

CallieRae: Madeline Green might not think I'm smart, but at least I'm smart enough to not wear my hair like an eighty-nine-year-old grandma. Puh-leeze. #MadelineMakesMyGrandmaLookHighFashion

MadelineG: Callie's talking about my hair? The girl looks like she shops out of a garbage Dumpster. What a loser! #CallieCreepsMeOut

Well, let's just say Madeline and Callie kept going . . . and it got worse. Soon all the secrets these two (former) best friends had were spread all over the Internet. Embarrassing photos were posted, rumors started, and feelings were hurt, hurt again, and then stepped on and hurt some more. My heart ached just reading the cruel posts.

There's nothing new about getting your feelings hurt. Even your great-great-aunt Eunice got into heated arguments with her best friend around the time cheese graters were invented. (Eugene informs me that Jeffrey Taylor created an early version of the grater in the 1920s by using the holes in a metal shower drain.[1] Yum. *Not really.*)

The difference is that Aunt Eunice and her friend might have said a mean comment or two, but they said those things to each other. Nobody else got caught up in the argument. And eventually, the two friends talked things out, exchanged apologies, and forgot the mean words.

That's sort of the way Jesus said to handle problems with our friends:

> *If your brother sins against you, go and show him his fault, just between the two of you. If he listens to you, you have won your brother over. But if he will not listen, take one or two others along, so that "every matter may be established by the testimony of two or three witnesses." If he refuses to listen to them, tell it to the church. (Matthew 18:15-17)*

Of course, the Internet didn't exist in Jesus' day. But His instructions are clear: handle your problem face-to-face. By talking things out with as few people as possible, you may keep emotions from escalating.

Today when we take our anger online, the results can blow up in our faces. Everyone you're connected with sees these emotional outbursts, and they can share them with their friends. The photos you post become public property and can be shared on other sites. The secrets you reveal can't be taken back—ever. What you say online can be shared and reshared months after you post it (and wish you hadn't).

When you vent your frustrations on the Internet, you pull other people into the conflict. If your friends see that you're upset, they get angry too . . . and they don't even know what they're angry about! They weren't part of the problem to begin with, so they probably won't be part of the solution. Instead, their comments may add fuel to an already potentially explosive situation. A simple misunderstanding between friends can quickly become an online riot. So really, what is the benefit in telling everyone how we feel?

Don't get me wrong. Your feelings are important. Anger, fear, giddiness, frustration, discouragement, and sadness are all important emotions to express—in healthy ways. So although we don't want to stifle our emotions, we *do* need to be wise with how we release them and who we release them to.

All Shook Up

Think of your feelings as being sealed inside a can of soda. When you get angry or hurt, it's like the can is being shaken up. You know what happens next, right?

The pressure builds.

You need to let out all those strong feelings, or you'll explode. You have *got* to talk to someone.

So you crack the can a little—just a smidge—and *whooooosh* . . . a fountain of soda bursts out in a geyser of fizzy frustration.

Posting your feelings online for the world to see (and judge) is rarely (make that *never!*) the best way to release those emotions. But you can't keep them inside either. So our group of wise young women have some ideas for healthy sharing:

Olivia: Sometimes when I need to let something out, I'll go in the backyard and scream really loudly, or I'll let myself have a good cry. Life seems more manageable once I let out my emotions.

Emily: I have a few close friends I trust. I'm careful not to start gossiping about others, and these friends hold me accountable. I know I can call them or talk to them at school when something's bothering me.

Penny: I journal a lot. That way I can write down all my frustrations on a piece of paper, and no one else ever needs to see it.

Camilla: I like to talk things through with my mom. She might not always know exactly what to do, but she'll listen to me for as long as I need. Somehow that always makes me feel better.

Katrina: I converse most regularly with Eugene to help me process things. But I also appreciate talking with Joanne Allen. Having an older mentor in my life helps me put things in perspective . . . and not overreact. I always feel better after she prays with me.

Tamika: I tell God what's hurting me. Sometimes it's crying into my pillow and talking to Him at the same time. I know it matters to God how I'm feeling, and that makes me feel better.

Here's a Secret...

I don't do just one thing to handle my hurts. I do *everything* these young ladies do. I talk to Whit (my mentor). I journal. I cry. I pray. As much as your parents and your best friends love you, God cares for you even more. He wants to know your hurts and fears. First Peter 5:7 (NLT) says to "give all your worries and cares to God, for he cares about you." And in Psalm 56:8 (NLT), David wrote, "You keep track of all my sorrows. You have collected all my tears in your bottle. You have recorded each one in your book."

Think about that: God keeps track, collects, and records your sadness. He wants you to give Him all your cares and worries. That doesn't sound like a God who would tell you to "just pull it together!" Those aren't God's words at all. He made you full of emotions. You can trust that your concerns, fears, and disappointments matter deeply to God. You are His beloved daughter.

So before you post your feelings on social media, ask yourself if it would be more helpful to share those things with God instead.

WHEN YOU'RE JUST LIKE A SHAKEN CAN OF COKE

Remember Who's Watching

People have lost their jobs, lost their friends, and lost the respect of their loved ones because of things they've decided to share online. You might be surprised at how a thoughtless post can get you in trouble. Penny can tell you about her friend . . .

Penny's Story

I had a friend who was a really nice person, but she tried to be ubercool on her Facebase page. She shared some not-so-appropriate jokes and used questionable language. She didn't think much about it until she received a letter from the college admissions office at the school she'd hoped to attend, with news that she'd been declined as a student.

Maria had really set her hopes on attending that school. She'd visited several times and had even developed a relationship with one of the admissions officers.

"Can you please tell me why I didn't get in?" Maria

asked when she called him. "I did well on my tests. I've worked hard on my GPA. What's the reason?"

The admissions officer stumbled over his words for a bit but finally relented. "The truth is your application was very impressive. But then one of our staff went on your Facebase page, and that was less so."

Maria gulped. She never imagined they'd check her page!

The admissions officer continued. "It became quite clear that you wouldn't be a very good fit for this school."

There was nothing Maria could do. The evidence glared from her screen.

It's pretty common for universities and potential employers to check out an applicant's online activity. After all, a social-media site can often give them a more honest portrayal of a person than the three questions she answered during an official interview.

All Your Friends in One Hallway

Have you ever been giggling with your friends when a teacher walked by? Do you stop talking or change the subject? Even if your conversation is completely innocent—like planning for the test tomorrow or the game on Friday—*how* you talk changes depending on your audience. You would probably speak differently to the principal of your school than to your little brother, even if you're talking about the same thing. For example, if you're in the school hallway looking outside during a big snowstorm and your principal walks up, you might say, "Good morning, Mr. Smith. Do you think we'll have a snow day tomorrow?" But if it's your little brother, you may yell, "Woo-hoo! Snow day tomorrow. I call the sled!"

When you're online, you have no idea who's "walking by." Although you might picture your buddies enjoying your observation about your math teacher's tacky tie, they won't be the only ones who see your comment. Imagine yourself surrounded by your aunt Edna, your youth-group leader, and—*gulp*—that math teacher's daughter when you write something.

Also keep in mind that online friends are very different from real-life friends. It's kinda like calling that squirty cheese in a can "real cheese." It's not the same—not at all. So remember, anything you post will be read by people you know well and trust, but it will also be seen by a lot of acquaintance-type people who aren't trustworthy at all and may spread around what you say.

Positive Postings

Although some feelings are best divulged to a worthy few, there are other situations when it's entirely appropriate to share with the world. Here's what the girls have to say about that:

CAMILLA: I posted a bunch of photos from our trip to Kenya last year. I thought everyone should be aware of the struggles the rest of the world faces and see what they can do to help.

EMILY: Yesterday on Club Kidchat, I asked, "Does anyone know where I can get a quality but inexpensive fingerprinting kit?" Several people had some good ideas, and one person said she owned one but never used it. She offered it to me for free!

PENNY: I love to paint. The other day I painted an abstract piece titled *Wooton with a Lemur and a Sock*. It had nothing to do with Wooton at all, except I let him name it. I posted a picture of it online to let people know it's for sale. No one's responded yet, but I'm not worried. Who doesn't like abstract art?

OLIVIA: Sometimes I'll watch a video that really makes me laugh (like the one where the cat plays the saxophone—hysterical!). Other videos make me tear up because they're so beautiful (like the one about the poodle who rescued his goat friend from a burning barn). I love sharing these videos to see what other people think of them.

TAMIKA: I love sharing photos. It's fun hearing what my friends think of the silly pictures I take. (My mom always gives me the okay *before* I post them. It's fun getting her comments too.)

KATRINA: I use my Facebase account to alert people to events and activities they should be informed about. Like last weekend at Whit's End, there was a fund-raiser for this medical ministry to developing countries called Samaritan's Purse. It's such a great cause!

If you need some help deciding what's good to post and what's not, here's a handy-dandy checklist:

To Share or Not to Share . . .
(Be sure you can answer "yes" to question #1. All other answers should be "no." If not, do not post.)

	Yes	No
1. Do I have my privacy settings set?	☐	☐
2. Is this something that would hurt someone else?	☐	☐
3. Is this something I'd be embarrassed for my grandma to see?	☐	☐
4. Will I regret posting this tomorrow after I've calmed down?	☐	☐
5. Does this reveal any personal information I wouldn't want a stranger to know? (Even with privacy settings, others can share with their own network, so people you don't know might still see it.)	☐	☐

	Yes	No

6. Does this go against what the Bible says in Philippians 4:8? ("Whatever is true, whatever is noble, whatever is right, whatever is pure, whatever is lovely, whatever is admirable . . . think about such things.") ☐ ☐

7. Is there anything about this post that makes me hesitate to share it? (If you answer "yes" to this question, you can double-check with a parent or wise friend to see what he or she thinks.) ☐ ☐

A Parker Pact

I was having dinner with the Parker family the other night. (Eva makes the most amazing enchiladas.) The kids—Olivia, Matthew, and Camilla—were peppering their parents with loads of questions, mainly about stuff going on online.

"Can I sign up for this online mystery newsletter?"

"Can I video-chat with Allison tonight?"

"Can I play on the computer after dinner?"

"Can I start a blog with my friends?"

"Can I friend Melissa's cousin in Albuquerque?"

"Can I get a pet llama?"

Eva tried to field all the questions. "No, no, absolutely not, yes, no, no."

David did his best as well. "Yes, no, if you're done with your homework, no, depends, yes."

"Did you say no or yes to Olivia's question, David?" Eva asked.

"Do you mean the second no or the third no?" David said.

"I don't know, but I think you no-ed one of my yeses," Eva responded.

"I was yes-ed," Olivia said. "You can't change your minds."

Camilla laughed. "They can do whatever they want . . . They're parents."

Obviously there was a lot of confusion. And somewhere in there, I'm pretty sure Camilla was given permission to get a llama. *Poor thing* . . . the llama, that is. The conversation ended with a brilliant suggestion from David.

"Let's just make up a family contract that says what everybody can and can't do online and with technology," he said.

Eva thought that was a great idea.

The next week when the Parkers came into Whit's End for ice cream, I asked them what they came up with. Olivia pulled a laptop out of her backpack and opened up a document.

"We worked on this together," she said. "And came up with something we all could agree to."

I thought it looked pretty good, so I asked if I could share it with you.

PARKER FAMILY TECHNOLOGY PACT

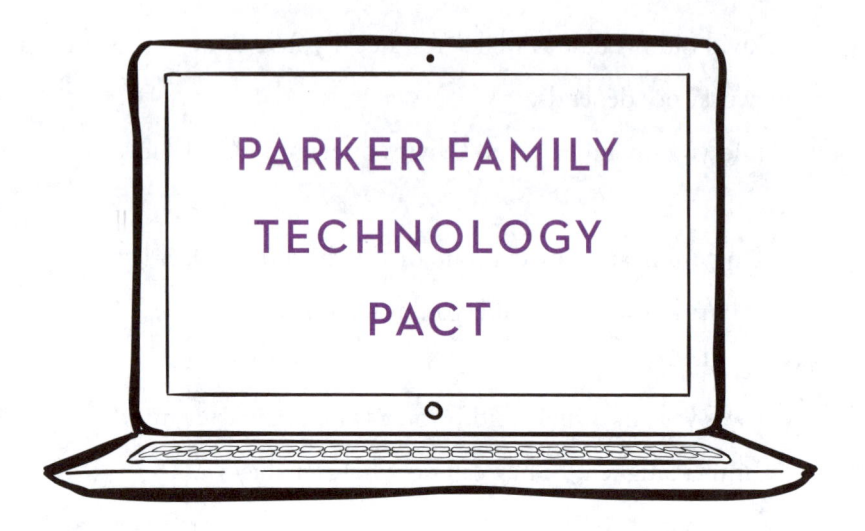

We, the Parker family, believe that we should glorify God in whatever we do—which includes how we use technology. We want to honor Him with our time, our words, and our thoughts.

Therefore, we agree to the following:
- I will not post things that are embarrassing or hurtful to someone else.
- I will not spread gossip.
- I will not watch or read things that dishonor God.
- I will unfriend/unfollow someone who shares questionable images or inappropriate language.
- I will only invite and accept friends whom I personally know.
- I will not agree to meet in person with anyone I've met online unless my parents know and are there.
- I will not post videos or photos without showing my parents first.
- I will not give out any personal info about my phone number and address or where I go to school.

- I will not download images without permission.
- I will not answer messages from people I don't know.
- I will have Dad help me set privacy settings on any account I set up.
- I will immediately show my parents a message from a stranger, or messages that are obscene, violent, or bullying.
- I will only go to websites that have been previously approved by my parents.

Additionally, we don't want our use of technology to interfere with quality time with our family and with God. So we acknowledge that . . .

- device use will be limited, unless we have been given special permission.
- devices will not be used during dinnertime or family time (parents included).
- devices will be charged at night in the dining room so we won't be tempted to use them after bedtime.
- all passwords and accounts must be shared with Mom and Dad.

If anyone is found in violation of these standards, the following will occur:

- First violation: Loss of devices for twenty-four hours.
- Second violation: Loss of devices for one week.
- Third violation: Loss of devices for two weeks, and you must clean the garage. Even Dad's greasy tool bench.

Signed,

David   *Eva*   *Matthew*
Olivia   *Camilla*

Your Turn

Talk to your family about creating a technology pact. Look at the pact the Parker family uses. It might not be the perfect plan for you, but it might give you some ideas of what yours could look like. Once you and your parents agree on the pact, print it out and have everybody sign it.

Chapter 9

Aaaack! Look at Me!
Texting Troubles

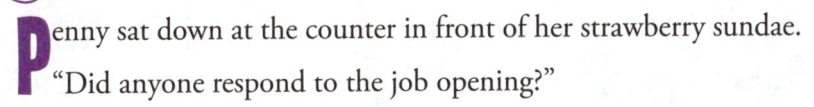

Penny sat down at the counter in front of her strawberry sundae. "Did anyone respond to the job opening?"

I nodded. We'd recently decided to hire some extra help at Whit's End. Whit put me in charge of going through applications and interviewing potential employees. Pretty cool, huh?

"I got a response from a pretty promising candidate," I said. "We've been texting back and forth the last couple days. She's smart and funny and thoughtful. I think she'll be great."

"Are you interviewing her?" Penny asked.

"Yep. She should be here any minute. Her name is Chloe."

Just then the door opened, and a cute teen girl with brown, curly hair stepped inside.

The girl, who was staring at her phone, walked to the counter and quickly glanced up.

"Hi, I'm Chloe," she said before looking right back at her phone.

"Um . . . well, I'm Connie. It's great to meet you!" I held out my hand to shake hers, but she didn't even notice. After an awkward moment, I put down my hand and invited her to sit at a table.

"Have a seat," I said. "Do you want anything to eat or drink? It's on the house."

Chloe sat down. Suddenly she started laughing.

"Is it something I said?" I asked.

"No," Chloe mumbled, still not looking up. "It's my friend Jayna."

I gave Penny a "What am I supposed to do now?" look. Penny responded with an apologetic "I have no idea" shoulder shrug. I sat down across from Chloe and asked a few questions. Her responses were okay, but she never looked me in the eye, and she mumbled her answers. I got the impression she wished she could be anywhere other than interacting with kids in an ice-cream shop.

After Chloe left, I walked over to Penny.

"It's like she could only interact through texting," I said. "In person, she didn't know how to make eye contact and speak clearly."

"And she totally left you hanging when you went to shake her hand," Penny added.

I know not every avid texter is as extreme as Chloe, but it did make me worry about the girls in my group. Were they texting so much that they might forget how to interact in person?

Perplexed by Text?

Living online—whether through your phone or your laptop—doesn't give you the chance to practice important life skills. Face-to-face communication is very different from text-to-text. With texts, all you have are the words. But when you talk in person, you communicate with your words, body language, facial expressions, and eyes.

I asked the girls if they've noticed the Chloe phenomenon in any of their friends. They all agreed they had a few friends who stared at their phones so much that the tops of their heads were more recognizable than their faces.

"It's sort of like texting requires a whole new set of rules," Tamika said.

"What do you mean?" I asked.

"We all know not to chew with our mouths full or interrupt people, but not everyone knows when it's rude to text or play on an app."

"So if you were writing the rules of cell phones," I said, "what would you suggest?"

Tamika: Never text while you're talking to someone. It's rude to have a text conversation with someone when you're having a live conversation with me. When you're looking at your phone, it makes me feel like you're not listening.

Olivia: Please, please turn off your phone when you're at the movies, at a play, or in church. Nobody wants to hear constant buzzing and beeping.

Penny: If you take a photo of me with your phone, please don't share it online or send it to someone else without first making sure it's okay with me. I hate it when I get online and suddenly there's a picture of me with cheese on my face and Jell-O in my hair.

Katrina: Don't text or play with your phone during school. I've had to confiscate a number of phones during my classes. It makes me—and other teachers I know—feel disrespected when students don't pay attention. That puts us in a bad mood. And teachers in bad moods give more pop quizzes.

EMILY: Never, ever forward texts I send you without getting my permission.

This is all great advice. But tagging on to what Emily said, make sure that your texts don't put others down and won't embarrass you later. Follow the same guidelines we talked about regarding social media. Texts can gain a life of their own if they get forwarded a bunch. So if you're angry, think carefully before hitting Send.

Here's a Secret...

Some parents want to read all the texts their children send and receive. And that's okay. Parents naturally want to protect their children. Many times once your parents see that you and your friends are sending respectful texts (and not texting at all hours), they'll check less frequently. The secret is that there are no secrets when it comes to texting. If you have a smartphone, ask your parents if there's anything they're concerned about with your habits. It's important to get those expectations out in the open and to keep the lines of communication open.

Smartphone Takeover

When I moved to Odyssey, almost nobody had a cell phone. Now it seems like everybody has one. I had Eugene look up some statistics for me. He said that in 1996 just over forty-four million people used cell phones in the United States. By 2010, that number had grown to more than three hundred million.[1] Today there are approximately seven billion active cell phones, which is also about the same number of people on the planet.[2] That's a huge number!

Of course, that doesn't mean everybody has a cell phone. Morgan from Holland, Michigan, e-mailed in to say,

> **Q:** My parents won't let me get a cell phone yet, even though a lot of my friends have them. They also won't let me sign up on any social-media sites. I feel so out of touch. How can I convince them that I need my own phone and some freedom on the computer?
> #CandidConversationsWithConnie

It can really be a struggle when it seems like everyone else is plugged in except you. Phones and other devices have become a kind of status symbol. So if you're deviceless, it can feel like you're missing out. But just because the trend is toward younger and younger kids getting cell phones, that isn't necessarily a good thing. In fact, the more you can stay away from getting a device, the better off you'll be.

Trust your parents on this one. Enjoy life—a *real*, face-to-face life, not one lived on a device.

I hope all this talk about cell phones and being online doesn't make you feel like that's where you need to be. The reason I'm spending all this time on it is because I want you to think ahead. *What kind of device user do you want to be?* Hopefully, you won't make a lot of the mistakes I did. Penny did a better job, but she still had her ups and downs. Here's her story . . .

Penny's Story

Connie and I decided to study the prophet Isaiah together. I like Isaiah. I mean, what's not to like about a guy who comes up with names like Maher-shalal-hash-baz for his kid. (Try monogramming *that* on a baseball cap.) But as

I started reading my Bible, my phone honked. (I've set it to "clown" mode.) The message was a joke from Wooton, so I texted him back. And since I had my phone in my hand, I thought I'd check my Facebase page. One of my friends had posted a music video she liked, so I started listening to it. That got me dancing around the room, so I did a search for "groovy new moves." Autocorrect must have changed *groovy* to *gravy*, because up popped a list of Thanksgiving recipes instead. *Hmmm,* I thought, *it'd be fun to cook something new.* So I started reading some cooking blogs. While I was deciding between a pecan-crusted cheesecake and kumquat pudding, Connie called.

"What did you think of Isaiah this morning?" she asked.

Oh yeah. Isaiah.

Connie talked about how she loved the way Isaiah listened to God, and how it challenged her to be obedient to what God has called her to do. That sounded way more profound than kumquat pudding.

Immediately I knew what I needed to do. I turned off my phone. Then I hid it under the couch cushions. And you know what? I enjoyed some uninterrupted time studying God's Word and talking to Him. He has some great posts in the Bible to "like" and "share." But I needed to shut off my phone to see it.

For all of you, whether you have a phone, a tablet, or a family-shared laptop, allow yourself time to be disconnected. Even Jesus took time away from crowds to pray and recharge (Luke 5:16).

Life is full of *noise*—and I don't mean dogs howling or Penny singing (although those two things usually go hand in hand). We're bombarded with information. Music in the car, commercials on TV, billboards beside the road. Add to that the texts, e-mails, pop-up ads, blogs, and myriad other websites you can see on your phone. God gave us pretty amazing brains that can handle all the information. The problem is, we were also made for times of silence. For being quiet.

When we go to sleep with our earbuds in and check our phones every time they buzz, we're not allowing for quiet. Take time to give your mind a chance to daydream, be creative, really relax, and most important, connect with God. There's a reason the psalmist wrote, "Be still, and know that I am God" (Psalm 46:10). Because sometimes it's in the stillness that we experience Him best.

Your Turn

Have a discussion with your friends and agree on a cell-phone pact. Make sure everyone understands that any pictures taken of you shouldn't be shared unless you give the okay. That goes for any messages you send too. Make agreements regarding spreading rumors or gossiping—and hold each other accountable. The Bible tells us to "put off falsehood and speak truthfully" about each other, "for we are all members of one body" (Ephesians 4:25). That verse is a great one to remember when it comes to your texting life.

Once you write up your cell-phone pact, print off enough copies for your friends and, with your parents' approval, have everybody sign it.

Chapter 10

Chickens on a Keyboard
Cyberbullying Stinks

Tamika slid into a seat across the counter from me at Whit's End. "I'm being bullied."

Penny and I groaned in unison. We knew how that felt. And we had ideas to deal with the situation.

"Ignore them," I said.

"Avoid them," Penny said.

"Speak up for yourself," I said.

"Stock up on those little tubes of chocolate-chip cookie dough," Penny said.

"What?" I asked.

She shrugged. "Well, it always makes *me* feel better."

I smiled. "First, let's try to actually stop the bullying. Who is it anyway?"

"That's the thing," Tamika said. "I don't know."

Penny and I exchanged glances.

"Is this one of those imaginary enemies, like some people have imaginary friends?" Penny asked. "Because when I had mine, I just imaginarily used some karate moves on them, and then everything was okay."

"This is a very real bully." Tamika handed over her phone. "I don't recognize the number, but look at my texts."

I scanned the screen, swallowing back my anger. Whoever this person was, she was sending some hateful and mean comments to Tamika. It made my stomach churn so badly, I couldn't read more than the first few texts.

Penny read these same comments over my shoulder. "That makes me so mad!" she said. "I wish my karate moves weren't just imaginary."

"That's not even the worst part," Tamika said. "Whoever this is also went to my Club Kidchat page and left terrible comments about me." Her eyes began to fill with tears. "There's nothing I can do!"

Unfortunately, Tamika's experience isn't unique. Online

bullying—also known as cyberbullying—is extremely common. In 2012, seven million families experienced verbal abuse just from Facebook users. This included being bullied, harrassed, or threatened.[1]

Cyberbullies usually use bad language, accusations, cruel statements, rumors, lies, or ugly pictures to torment you. This can often be more traumatic than a regular schoolyard bully because everyone can see what's being posted about you. Hundreds or thousands of people are able to read posts or see comments made in chat rooms or online forums.

The problem is, online bullying is easy. Someone can set up a fake profile or text from an unknown phone number, which makes it difficult to find out who's doing the bullying. Online bullies are cowards. Maybe the ultimate cowards, because they hide behind a user name and spew their hurtful words. I sort of picture them like a chicken pecking away on a keyboard!

If you're the victim of cyberbullying, you can do some things to combat it. I had a chat with Detective Polehaus at the Odyssey Police Department, and these are some tips he gave me:
- Learn to block people from e-mail, social-media sites, or texting. You have control over your settings, so use them. If you start receiving disturbing messages—even one—you can keep them from showing up again.

- Use the highest privacy settings. Most social-media users don't adjust their privacy settings, which means practically anyone can get on their pages to read postings or view photos. Make certain only your friends can see your page. And make sure your "friends" are real friends. Don't accept friend requests from people you don't personally know and trust.
- Don't reply to any message that is abusive or obscene. If you continually receive threatening or mean messages, save them in a file without reading them. This is helpful if things get so out of hand that you want to go to the police and press charges. Cyberbullying is against the law.
- Tell your parents. Many kids worry that their parents will take away their phones or computers, so they keep the bullying to themselves. It's much smarter to get your parents involved right away so they can help you figure out the best way to handle these attacks.
- If you are ever threatened physically, report it to the police. If the bullying takes place on a website, have your parents contact the website host to request that the comment be removed. If someone asks you to share an inappropriate picture, report that person right away to your parents and the police.

- Only share your password with your parents. The fewer people who have access to your account, the better.

Olivia learned that last one the hard way. She'll tell you about it.

Olivia's Story

My friend Zoe and I shared just about everything: shoes, sweaters, hair products, and pizza on Friday night. So it seemed totally natural for her to have the password to my Club Kidchat account. After all, I used the same password everywhere, and she knew pretty much everything about me. It wasn't a problem—until we got in a fight. Suddenly this friend I totally trusted was posting updates and photos on *my* account. She said awful things—and other people thought it was *me* saying them. Talk about embarrassing! Eventually my parents talked to hers, and we got it worked out. She even apologized to me, and we're friends again. But I can't take back what other people saw or change what they think of me now. Zoe and I both updated our passwords and agreed that even though we'll still share lip gloss, we're keeping our passwords to ourselves.

Olivia's right. I mean, if everyone knew my password was WodFamChocSod7, they'd be getting into my account and saying things like "Free ice cream at Whit's End. I'm buying!" or "I'm so in love with Jeff Lewis" (neither is true, by the way).

Oh, wait. I just realized I need to change my password. Forget that one I just said. It's different now. Really.

Here's a Secret...

Try to make your password something people wouldn't guess. Don't use your name, birthday, pet's name, or obvious numbers (like 12345). Those are things people often try if they want to break into your account. Here are some tips for creating unique passwords that you can still remember:

- The longer the password, the harder it is to crack. Make your passwords at least twelve characters.

- Use a combination of upper- and lowercase letters, numbers, and symbols. Substitute a zero for an *o*, an "@" for an *A*, or a "$" for an *S*.
- Take a sentence and create it into a password. For example, I could take the first letter of the lyrics to "Jesus Loves Me" and make it into a password like this: JLMtikFTBtm$L1. Get it? Favorite verses with extra exclamation points also make great passwords, like Ephesians2:10!

Listen Up

One final thought about cyberbullying. It sort of goes back to what I told Tamika at the beginning of this chapter. When it comes to bullies, it's often best to ignore them and speak up for yourself.

I talked a lot about bullies in *Candid Conversations with Connie, Vol. 2*, so I'll be brief (at least as brief as I can be) here. Bullies win when you stay quiet about the abuse and listen to what they say. Instead of listening to their negative words, tune in to the life-giving words of your heavenly Father:

You are the apple of His eye (Psalm 17:8).

You are wonderfully made (Psalm 139:14).

You are His child (John 1:12).

You are His friend (John 15:15).

You are a conqueror (Romans 8:37).

You have been blessed with spiritual blessings (Ephesians 1:3).

You are His workmanship, created to do good (Ephesians 2:10).

When you truly understand what God says about you, a bully's comments won't drag you down. Then you can go on the offensive and stand up to the bully by telling your parents and friends what's happening. Lies and rumors about you carry a lot less power when the people you love know the truth and support you.

Your Turn

So now that we've talked about all things Internet, you can take this quiz to see how online savvy you are:

1. You have Internet rules at your house, but your friend's parents aren't as strict. So when you're at her house, you . . .
   A. go with her parents' rules instead. Her house, her rules. Right?
   B. stick with the rules your parents gave you.

2. You're checking your e-mail and see a message from your Internet provider that says something is wrong with your account. They need your password to fix it. You . . .
   A. reply and send your password. Surely you can trust your Internet provider.
   B. don't send anything. You never tell anyone your password, even if they say something needs to be fixed.

3. You just found out your best friend has spread an awful rumor about you online, and you're livid. So you . . .
   A. get online and start posting her darkest secrets. Two can play at this game.
   B. take some time to cool off and give her a call to find out what happened.

4. You've been playing this online game for a while. Recently you met a girl named Bailey. She's your age and seems really nice. She suggests that you meet at a coffee shop this weekend. Do you do it?
   A. Sure. She seems like she could be a really good friend.
   B. Nope. But I do tell my parents. You never know who you're really talking to online.

5. You start getting crude texts from a number you don't know. You . . .
   A. text back to find out who it is.
   B. block future texts. You don't need to put up with that.

6. You often check out a website that sells really cool shoes. One time you get a pop-up box saying you can enter a contest for "free shoes for life!" You just need to send in your name and cell-phone number. You . . .
   A. give them the information, of course. Who wouldn't want free shoes!?
   B. check with your parents first. You might just be putting yourself on an annoying marketing list.

7. Someone at school posted an awful picture of you online and said how fat and ugly you are. You . . .
   A. continually check the site to see how many people have commented on it and "liked" it.
   B. talk to your parents and come up with a plan to contact the poster's parents and have it removed. If that doesn't work, you go directly to the website to have the image taken down.

8. Someone contacts you saying she's "a friend of a friend." She wants to mail you something and asks for your home address. You . . .

   A. send your address. How fun that you're going to get mail!

   B. realize you have no idea who this person is, so you don't give out personal information.

9. You receive an e-mail from a modeling company that says you could be a real model! But it needs some more pictures to know for sure. They ask you to text them some. You . . .

   A. squeal with excitement and then snap a few selfies to send.

   B. don't send them anything. You never send photos to people you don't know. (And then you tell your parents about this fishy request.)

10. You're sitting in on a chat session when someone starts saying really mean things. You . . .

    A. respond with mean things of your own.

    B. don't respond at all.

11. You read an article online that says spreading peanut butter all over your face will get rid of zits forever. So you . . .

    A. go buy two big jars of peanut butter.

    B. laugh. You'll take medical advice from your doctor instead.

So you probably already figured out that the A answers are wrong and the B answers are right. In this case, it's better to be a B student. The Internet can be a helpful tool, or it can become a hazard. Use it wisely. Always be careful about what you post and who you send information to. Don't believe everything you read. And when in doubt, ask your parents.

Oh yeah, don't try that peanut-butter-on-your-face idea. It doesn't work . . . unless you're trying to get your dog to lick you.

Chapter 11

Remote-Controlled Adventures

Media Choices

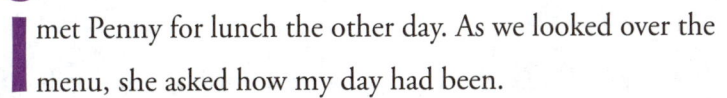

I met Penny for lunch the other day. As we looked over the menu, she asked how my day had been.

"Satisfactory," I told her.

She giggled.

I looked up from the menu. "And why do you chortle?"

She laughed harder.

"Penny! What is it?"

"It's pretty obvious you've been hanging around Eugene today."

I thought about it. "Well, yes. I was assisting him with the installation of the new sound system in the Little Theater at Whit's End. But how did you know?"

"Your vocabulary: 'satisfactory,' 'chortle,' 'assisting with the installation.'" She shook her head. "You sound just like him!"

"I didn't even notice."

"It's kind of like when you start talking in a British accent after we watch *Uptown Manor House*." She mimicked me. "Penny, would you be a love and fetch me a spot of tea?" For added effect, she stuck out her pinky while sipping her water.

"I guess you're right," I said with a laugh. "Sometimes a little exposure makes a big difference."

"Yep. Like a little Tabasco sauce in a big pitcher of lemonade tastes like a big pitcher of Tabasco," Penny said.

I raised my eyebrows, trying to figure out the connection. "What?" I said.

"Wooton and I were experimenting with making a hot-and-sour drink to go with our hot-and-sour soup," Penny explained. She looked out the window with a thoughtful stare. "Tabasco definitely didn't work. Maybe we could try some habanero peppers in grapefruit juice."

"Remind me to never let you make a Chinese dinner," I told her.

Sponge Brains

For weeks after my conversation with Penny, I thought about what my brain was soaking up. Every time I streamed music on my smartphone, I listened more closely to the lyrics. When I flipped through TV stations, I recognized more quickly when characters were being rude or crude. When I read reviews for upcoming movies, I looked more closely at questionable content.

If listening to Eugene changed the way I spoke, how were these messages impacting the way I acted? We're constantly receiving messages—even when we don't realize it. I hadn't tried to sound like Eugene (trust me, that's the *last* thing I'd want!), but my brain had absorbed his way of speaking. Without realizing it, I'd started to sound like a genius. But if song lyrics or movie dialogue seeped into the way I spoke, I'm guessing I wouldn't sound smart at all.

I asked the girls how the media has unknowingly affected them:

OLIVIA: I watched a movie where the family members spoke harshly to each other—calling each other names. It was a funny movie, but when I came home, I slipped and called my brother one of those names. I didn't mean to! It just came out.

CAMILLA: My friends convinced me to watch this scary movie. I didn't want them to think I was babyish, so I watched it.

I didn't like it at all. There were some pretty gross scenes that are now stuck in my head. I wish I could unsee them, but I can't.

TAMIKA: My cousin liked this really catchy song. I told her I didn't want to hear it, because the lyrics weren't great. She kept telling me that it's "just music," and you don't really hear what they're saying. We listened to the song a few times in her room and danced around. Later that day I noticed I was singing those lyrics to myself while I was setting the table. Yep. Those lyrics I supposedly wouldn't even hear . . . I heard them.

We underestimate what our subconscious minds pick up. The subconscious is the part of our brains that stores all the stuff we're not totally aware of. It's where dreams form and "forgotten" memories are remembered. Our subconscious sees and hears everything. (Well, maybe not *everything*. But a lot of stuff gets in our brains.) So even though we think, *I won't let this movie affect me*, or *I won't pay attention to the lyrics*, we can't really make that choice. Our brains soak it up anyway.

When you think about it, that's pretty amazing. (Yay, God, for making amazing brains!) But it's also kind of scary, because it means we need to be really careful about what we put in our brains.

Remember how we talked about how eating healthy foods

makes your body healthier and eating unhealthy foods makes you unhealthier? The same is true for your brain. Sodas and cookies hurt our bodies and make us feel sluggish and tired. We can't act the way God intended us to. In a similar way, a diet of unwholesome movies, music, and TV clogs up our brains. All of this media junk food affects the way we think and act. Simply put, when you put good stuff in your brain, good stuff comes out. When you put bad stuff in, bad things come out.

I love what the apostle Paul wrote in Colossians 3:2: "Set your minds on things above, not on earthly things." God entrusted us with amazing brains, and He wants us to use them for His glory. Later in the same chapter, Paul said to rid ourselves of anger, slander, filthy language, and lies (verse 8). We can't do that if our minds are filled with "earthly" entertainment. When I think about the songs on the radio or the shows on TV, a lot of popular ones are packed with filthy language.

I don't want that stuff in my brain. Just like I care for my body, I want to take care of my brain and feed it things that will help me focus on God.

Here are some ways you can join me in making sure you're putting "healthy food" in your mind when it comes to movies and media:

1. *Do your research.* Movie ratings can be helpful, but they don't always give you the whole picture. Try checking out reviews

on Christian websites like PluggedIn.com to get information on popular movies, music, and video games.

2. *Talk to your parents.* I know you'd rather not ask your parents, because they'll probably tell you not to watch all the shows everyone else is watching. But parents have rules for a reason. Emily has a great story about that.

Emily's Story

"C'mon, Mom. Please!" I begged.

"Emily! I've told you already, your dad and I don't want you watching that movie. Please stop asking." My mom looked at me pointedly, and I knew I'd better stop whining. But it wasn't fair. All my friends were going to see the new film *Spies and Lies*—and I was dying to go with them.

"But what am I going to do at home by myself?" I asked.

"You could clean out the toilets." She smiled.

I groaned.

"Or you could read *Spies and Lies* instead." She handed me a book sitting on the coffee table. "I picked it up from the library for you."

I thanked her. But inside I thought, *It's a book. I won't be able to see the explosions and big-name actors that are in the movie.*

Five hours later, I finally put down the book and ran to find my mom.

"That was awesome," I said. "Thanks!" (And this time I meant it.) The ending of the book had really surprised me. Who would've expected a twin brother working as a double agent for the enemy?

I dialed my friend Alisha to talk about the movie. She hadn't been as impressed with the movie as I had been with the book.

"Kendra fell asleep because the movie just dragged," she said. "Some of the fight scenes were really gross. I couldn't even watch those parts, and there were a lot of them."

Strange, I thought. I hadn't remembered many fight scenes in the book. "But what about when the main character reunites with his twin brother at the end?" I asked.

Alisha had no idea what I was talking about.

> "Nothing like that happened in the movie. The spy just blazed into the sunset with a girl on his speedboat."
>
> Wow, I thought, *they really missed out on a good mystery.*
>
> I'm still interested in seeing movies, of course, but now I'm thinking I might start making more trips to the library.

While you're talking with your parents about good shows to watch, ask about some of their favorite movies. You could even suggest gathering everybody together for a movie night with a family-friendly film. (See "Your Turn" at the end of this chapter for ideas.)

3. *Check your spirit.* If you're a Christian, the Holy Spirit resides within you. When you feel that little, uncomfortable gnawing as you're watching a movie, it could be God's Spirit telling you that this content isn't okay to put in your brain. Pay attention to that feeling. If you need to walk out of the theater, do it. (Some movie theaters will even refund your money if it's still during the first half of the film.) When you recognize that what you're watching isn't very good "soul" food, be strong. Turn it off. Change the channel. Stand up and tell your friends, "I don't feel good about watching this. Can we do something else?"

Here's a Secret...

Some of the best conversations I've had with my friends have started after a good movie. Take time after watching a movie to talk about it. Here are some conversation starters:

- What did you like about the main character?
- What would you do the same or differently if you found yourself in this situation?
- Did this movie change your thoughts on any situations you're currently going through?

Live Your Own Adventure

We once did a KYDS Radio show about a boy named Joey who developed an obsession with his computer, Hallie. She became alive to him and slowly demanded more and more of his time. Eventually he spent his entire day in his room. He ignored his friends and family and all the activities he used to enjoy. His *virtual* life became more comfortable than his *real* life.*

---

* Want to hear more of Joey's story? Go to WhitsEnd.org and search for the Adventures in Odyssey radio drama "My Girl Hallie," episode 537, album 41, *In Hot Pursuit*.

This may sound like a far-out story, but the truth is, it's pretty easy to get addicted to watching TV, playing video games, surfing the net, or going to movies. Having adventures through a TV detective is easier than going outside and creating our own excitement, but easy doesn't equal better.

God designed us for adventure, romance, laughter, relationship, and excitement. (Did you really think Hollywood made those up?) He put those desires in our hearts when He created us. And do you know why we cheer when evil is defeated and good prevails? It's because God made us that way!

Moviemakers create only a shadow of those heart-stirring moments. God wrote the book on them. Because those desires live in each of us, we crave them like a hot-fudge sundae. We love to see the hero risk his life for the woman he loves or the superhero defeat the villain who wanted to take over the world. We love to laugh, to see beauty, and to sit on the edge of our seats wondering what's going to happen next. We love to cheer for the underdog who overcomes insurmountable obstacles to achieve her goal. We love all of these things because God put them in our hearts.

He has an adventure for you—a real-life, true adventure. Somewhere down the road, He has a romance for you too. And don't be surprised if you battle evil in one way or another at times in your life. God is your screenwriter . . . and He writes the best stories.

So enjoy the movies you watch, but don't trade your life for them. Don't become so immersed in TV, music, and even books that you miss out on the story God is writing in your life. The friendships, activities, and things He prompts your heart to do are all part of your *amazing* story.

Your Turn

Some Friday nights are just meant for a bunch of friends, a good movie, and a bowl of cookie dou— I mean, popcorn. And there are great movies out there.* Here are some the girls and I have really enjoyed. (Be sure to check with a parent first.)

Soul Surfer
Maleficent
Dolphin's Tale ✓
The Giver
Earth to Echo ✓
Akeelah and the Bee
Charlotte's Web (2006 version) ✓
City of Ember
The Book Thief
Hugo
Enchanted

---
* Special thanks to the guys at PluggedIn.com for this list.

The Odd Life of Timothy Green

Oz the Great and Powerful

Ramona and Beezus

Secret Garden (1949 version)

The Princess Diaries

Nim's Island

Watching a movie can also create some great family time . . . if you take time to discuss it afterward. Talk to your parents about watching some of their favorite classic movies. You may also want to view something together from our list.

During your discussion, ask your parents if they've ever seen your words or actions change because of something you saw in a movie or on a TV show. It's important to watch out for anything that can influence your life.

Chapter 12

Drowning in Honey
The Time of Your Life

The problem started with a Siamese cat in a stocking cap. (Cats in hats often mean big problems.)

"Come here, you've got to watch this." I told Eugene when he walked through the door at Whit's End.

"What, pray tell, is amusing you, Miss Kendall?" he asked, coming over to the counter. He didn't look ready to be amused.

"Watch this video," I said, pressing play on my laptop. Eugene looked over my shoulder and watched two minutes of kittens wearing hats. Clown hats. Chef hats. Gardening hats. Stocking caps. I have to admit, it was a little dumb. But for some reason, I laughed every time I watched it.

The video ended. I turned to Eugene, who rolled his eyes with such exasperation that his glasses nearly toppled off his face. "*That's* what I had to see? I've just wasted two minutes of my life, and I only receive roughly fifty-two million to begin with."

"It's just a couple of minutes," I muttered. "Lighten up."

"Life is lost in the minutes," Eugene told me definitely.

I shrugged.

"I think someone as intelligent as you could find better ways to occupy your time than hours of kitten videos," he added.

"Well, I've been meaning to start reading this book Whit gave me."

"An excellent use of time," Eugene said.

"And I'd like to be able to do one hundred sit-ups."

"Another fine endeavor."

"And I was thinking about working on a new vegan milkshake made from pine nuts and celery."

"Perhaps you should stick with those first two options."

Eugene went upstairs to work on the Imagination Station. I glanced at the clock and grimaced. Had I really just spent eighty minutes watching "cute" videos online? I closed my laptop and started thinking. Those kittens might have looked cute, but they were thieves—of my time!

I'm not the only one who spends a lot of time on my phone and computer. In my sociology class, the professor said kids between the ages of eight and eighteen spend more than seven hours in front of a screen every day—watching TV, playing video games, surfing the Internet, or texting.[1] That's a *lot* of time.

Time Well Spent

Imagine what we could do with an extra seven hours a day . . . which adds up to twenty-five hundred hours a year. We could become award-winning gymnasts. Or write a book. Or improve the lives of fifty people living in our neighborhoods. Or record a CD. Or earn scholarships for being excellent trombone players. The possibilities are endless.

Here are some examples of kids who did just that:

> In kindergarten, Olivia Bennett discovered she had cancer. Despite the difficult years of treatments and recovery at home, she pursued her passion for art. When she sold a painting for fifty dollars at age eight, she realized she might have a future in the field. She continued developing her painting skills and eventually opened a gallery at age fourteen. Olivia believes God

guides her art, but that doesn't make her lazy—it only makes her work harder. She sometimes works in her studio for six hours a day.[2]

Seventeen-year-old Chelsea Eubank was already struggling with a learning disability when her dad unexpectedly died. Instead of allowing her difficult life to sink her into self-pity, Chelsea threw herself into knowing God better. As a result, she wanted to express her faith in her clothing. But she couldn't find Christian clothes she liked. So Chelsea decided to create her own. She committed hours each day to experimenting with designing logos. Some worked. Others didn't. Eventually she launched a successful clothing line.[3]

Both Olivia and Chelsea committed their time to doing something they were passionate about. Were they on their smartphones or computers sometimes? I'm sure they were. But they didn't allow screens to take over their lives. And they didn't give up when life became difficult. Even when cancer, death, and discouragement entered the picture, they didn't resort to escaping from life by mindlessly channel surfing. They decided they were going to do something big, and they worked hard—*really* hard— to do it.

I'm not saying you need to start a clothing company in the

next three years. God might call you to do something totally different. But He does tell you in Ephesians 5:15-16 (ESV), "Look carefully then how you walk, not as unwise but as wise, making the best use of the time." God has given you time. Maybe you'll get fifty-two million minutes (or just under ninety-nine years), like Eugene expects. But no matter how much time God gives you, what matters is that you're wise with it.

God also gives you gifts and talents. Maybe they're obvious ones—like academics, athletics, or drama. Maybe they're less evident, like making people laugh or being inventive. Maybe you're still learning what they are. Just know that when you spend time cultivating those gifts, God can use you to accomplish amazing things.

The girls in Odyssey might not be selling their art for thousands of dollars, but they've done some pretty phenomenal things that have huge eternal rewards.

Olivia Parker helped me organize an Easter program at the community center in Connellsville. She spent countless hours writing the script, auditioning kids from Whit's End, painting sets, and creating costumes. More than five hundred people saw the show. Many of them didn't know much about Jesus but left understanding what He did for them.

Emily Jones has a problem-solving brain. Her perseverance in figuring out mysteries helped resolve a cheating scandal at school.

Another time, she and Matthew Parker figured out who robbed a convenience store.*

Tamika Washington volunteers with a Kids' Bible Club at the First Church of Odyssey. She leads songs, teaches Bible stories, and helps the kids learn verses. A lot of little kids know their Bibles better because of Tamika.

Matthew Parker designed a website for the local homeless center. Now volunteers can easily sign up to help, and other people can donate online. The center is receiving more volunteers and donations than ever. Countless families have found jobs and are now able to afford homes, in part because of Matthew's help.

It didn't take a lot of money or incredible talent to make these things happen. It just took people who decided they wanted to get away from their screens for a while and make a difference instead. (Except for Matthew, who was on a computer making the website . . . But you get my point.)

You Were Made for More

Satan will try to make you live small. He wants you to think that life is all about entertaining yourself. He'd love for you to spend hours Photoshopping selfies and updating your social-media

---

* Want to hear exactly how Emily and Matthew solved the cheating and robbery mysteries? Go to WhitsEnd.org and search for the Adventures in Odyssey radio dramas "Repent After Me," episode 732, album 57, *A Call to Something More*, and "The Case of the Ball Cap Hero," episode 786, album 60, *Head over Heels*.

accounts. He doesn't want you to do anything significant with your life—certainly nothing that will help others grow closer to God. Don't get me wrong: I don't think texting or being on a computer are of the devil. But I do believe those activities can rob us of time and cause us to live in a smaller story. As Penny showed me, too much of a good thing can actually be a bad thing.

Penny's Story

Penny came into Whit's End yesterday. Actually, "came into" wouldn't really be accurate. She bounced in on a pogo stick, yodeling "Jesus Loves Me." Then she did five pirouettes across the floor. Even for Penny, it seemed a bit over the top.

"Are you feeling okay?" I asked.

"I feel great!" she told me. "It must be the extra antioxidants. Can I have some coffee?"

"Um, I don't think you need it," I told her. "And what do you mean by extra antioxidants?"

"I was reading this article today that said coffee is good for you because it includes antioxidants that are superhealthy. So I decided to start drinking coffee even though I usually don't, because caffeine makes me shake like a bobblehead in an earthquake."

"How much coffee did you drink?"

Penny lifted up her hand and started checking off fingers, which appeared to be shaking involuntarily. "One at prebreakfast, one at breakfast, one at postbreakfast, one at brunch." She looked down at her fingers. "I don't think I have enough fingers. Or maybe I do. I can't tell when they don't stay still."

I suggested she go jump on a trampoline for a while... and not have any more coffee. *Ever.*

Proverbs 25:16 tells us, "If you find honey, eat just enough—too much of it, and you will vomit." That's pretty gross, but it's true. And it applies to honey and every other "good" thing—whether it's coffee or movies or posting on social media or playing Bitter Birds. Limit the time you spend on these activities. Don't let your time run away with you, because a life full of distraction leads to little action.

You aren't meant for a small story. You serve a big God who has given you skills and abilities because He has big things planned for you. When you settle for small goals—looking cute, being popular, not being bored, getting one hundred "likes" on your status—you set yourself up for a small life.

Don't fall for that lie! You can do all things through Christ (Philippians 4:13). Nothing is impossible when it's something God has called you to (Luke 1:37). So live a God-sized life.

It won't be easy. People may even discourage you from thinking big. Especially when you're young, people may tell you that you can't do anything really significant. Listen to this text I received from Braelynn in Raton, New Mexico:

> **Q:** I'd love to start a club at my high school where teens mentor girls in elementary school. I really could have used a program like this when I was younger. But the teachers and principal feel it's too much work when I'm "just a teenager." They won't even let me try. Are they right? Do I need to be older to do anything important? #CandidConversationsWithConnie

Braelynn, God *loves* using teenagers. Even if the rest of the world looks at you and says "you're too young," God doesn't see you that way. He says in 1 Timothy 4:12, "Don't let anyone look down on you because you are young, but set an example for the believers in speech, in life, in love, in faith and in purity."

For thousands of years, God has used teens to make huge impacts. Esther saved the Jewish race. Mary birthed and raised the Messiah. Joseph saved an entire region of the world from starvation. David killed a giant. And God *still* does big things through teenagers.

Your parents and teachers have more life experience than you, so they are a good source of advice. They know what mistakes you could make. Maybe you have a tendency to bite off more than you can chew. But that doesn't mean you should give up. Show them you're serious about your commitment. One way to do this would be to find a few other girls who are interested in your idea. Then get together and create a plan to make your club happen. Write out your goals and then share them with your teachers and principal to prove that you're committed to this idea.

Jordan from St. Louis, Missouri, wrote in with another question:

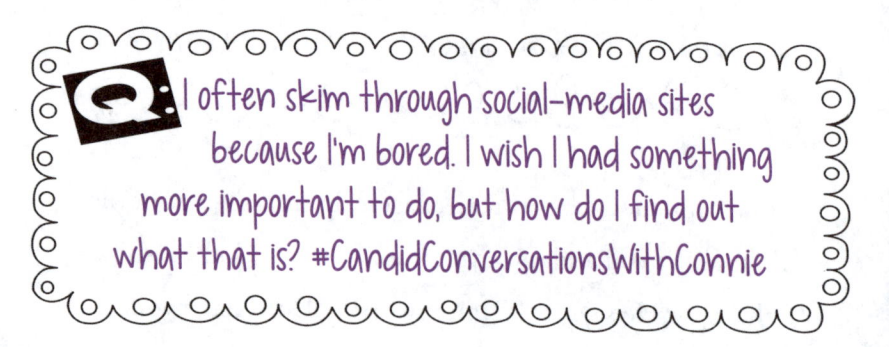

Q: I often skim through social-media sites because I'm bored. I wish I had something more important to do, but how do I find out what that is? #CandidConversationsWithConnie

It's a great question, Jordan. I'll let Penny give her input:

PENNY: Take time with God. Spend time praying and learning Scripture. Even though I'm a pretty social person, I hear God best when I'm not around anyone. There's this meadow I like to walk through just because it's where I feel close to Him. The more you know God, the better you'll learn to recognize His voice. Pay attention to those passions He puts on your heart and the natural skills He's given you. Do you like to write, sing, paint, or organize activities? The things you enjoy are often God-given talents that you can use to serve God and love others. Do you feel a burden for kids with disabilities, orphaned children in Bolivia, or that kid in your school who always looks lonely? Listen to that—it could be the Holy Spirit has given you a heart for those people.

Penny's right. When opportunities pique your interest, it could be God giving you a nudge to go for it. Maybe you've heard someone talk about the Humane Society or the choir at church needing volunteers and thought, *That sounds like fun.*

Even when we learn about opportunities to help, it's hard to follow through. But God shows us opportunities and gives us goals for a reason. I'll share a conversation I had with Camilla when she was setting goals for the year.

ME: Camilla, what are three things you'd like to do this year?

Camilla: Well, I love basketball, so I'd like to make the basketball team. And ever since we took that trip to Africa, I keep thinking about doing a fund-raising dinner at church to raise money to send those kids for schoolbooks. But that seems like a pretty big thing.

Me: It's okay to dream big. What's your third thing?

Camilla: I'm a pretty new Christian, and my mom and others have said reading through the Bible would really help me grow. So I'd like to read through the whole Bible in one year.

Me: Those are some great goals. So—and this is very important—write them down. Then hang them up somewhere so you'll be reminded of them every day. You can't accomplish these things in a day. But you can do a little each day to achieve your goals.

Camilla's Goals
1. Make the basketball team.
2. Organize a fund-raiser for kids in Kenya.
3. Read through the Bible.

CAMILLA: My goals still seem too big. I don't think I can do them.

ME: So try breaking them down into smaller goals. What steps do you need to take to make the basketball team?

CAMILLA: Well, I know I need to practice, but we don't even have a basketball hoop at home.

ME: So where could you get in some practice?

CAMILLA: I could practice dribbling in the driveway. And I know some girls play every Saturday at the playground. Maybe I could practice with them. They're older and pretty good, so I could learn a lot. And I should probably work on my endurance by running.

ME: Great. So your first goal breaks down into these four steps.

Make Basketball Team
1. Dribble in the driveway every day.
2. Practice Saturdays with older, more skilled players.
3. Ask for advice and tips from these girls.
4. Start running twice a week.

We broke the rest of Camilla's goals into bite-size pieces. Here's what we ended up with:

Organize Fund-raising Dinner for Kids in Kenya

1. Find friends who can be on a planning committee.
2. Talk to pastor and parents to get permission and set date.
3. Check with local restaurants to see if any would be willing to donate food.
4. Plan full menu based on donations.
5. Announce event at church, send out e-mails, and hang flyers.
6. Recruit more volunteers to help with serving, decorating, and cleanup.

Read Through Bible in a Year

1. Have Mom help me find a good daily-reading plan.
2. Find a Bible version I can easily understand.
3. Schedule a specific reading time each day, so I don't put it off. Maybe 7:00 to 7:30 a.m.
4. Find friend who will do it with me and can hold me accountable.
5. Set my alarm the night before so I wake up on time.

Once all of these goals were broken down into smaller pieces, Camilla saw they were all really doable. She's already started working on each of them . . . going step by step to get them done.

Your Turn

You knew this was coming, right? Spend some time in prayer about what goals you should make for this year. Jot them down. Beneath each goal, brainstorm the steps it will take to accomplish it. (Ask your parents for help, if you need it.) Then make a copy of your goals and post it where you'll see them every day.

My Goals

1. _____

Steps to take:

_____

_____

_____

_____

2. _____

Steps to take:

_____

_____

_____

3. _____

Steps to take:

_____

_____

_____

Here's a Secret...

Expect obstacles. Expect failures. Worthwhile goals are rarely easy to achieve. On some mornings, Camilla will likely hear her alarm and groan, *Why am I waking up this early?* She might have trouble finding friends who are willing to be on her committee to help kids in Kenya. She may realize she has little natural ability at playing basketball, and it's getting hot outside—too hot to go running. There will always be great reasons for giving up on your goals. You'll be tempted to quit, to just watch TV and live a mediocre life. Fight those feelings. Choose to keep working toward your goals. Even if you just shut off your alarm for an entire week and are way behind on your Bible reading, remind yourself that your goals matter. Pray for strength and then start again. You can do it!

A Final Note

I may not know you personally. Maybe I've served you a raspberry-ripple sundae at Whit's End. Or perhaps I've never had the privilege of sitting across from you and hearing all about your life. But whether I know you or not, I *do* know the God who made you. And I know the kind of people He creates. He doesn't make "practice" people. It's not like He knits somebody together, shakes His head, and thinks, *Oh well, I'll do better with the next one.* Nope. He creates each person beautiful, and with a purpose and a plan.

That means *you* are beautiful. *You* have a purpose and a plan. God's written out the moments of your life. He catches your tears. He delights in you and sings over you. He doesn't just love you with a love you can't fathom; He really, really *likes* you too.

So don't let those minutes He gives you wash away into nothingness. Each moment on this earth is a gift. Each one has a purpose.

Thanks for hanging out with me and my friends! It's been super fun for us, and I hope you feel the same way.

Look at the time—we missed the movie! But you know what? I don't care. I'd much rather hang out with my friends and talk about real life.

Come on, girls! Let's get another round of marshmallow-and-coconut sundaes.

Notes

Chapter 1
1. American Society for Aesthetic Plastic Surgery, "The American Society for Aesthetic Plastic Surgery Reports Americans Spent Largest Amount on Cosmetic Surgery Since the Great Recession of 2008," news release, March 20, 2014, http://www.surgery.org/media/news-releases/the-american-society-for-aesthetic-plastic-surgery-reports-americans-spent-largest-amount-on-cosmetic-surger.

Chapter 2
1. According to scientists, two trillion cells are created every day, which breaks down to a little over 23 million cells per second. See "Building Blocks of Life," Arizona State University School of Life Sciences, accessed June 24, 2015, http://askabiologist.asu.edu/content/cells-divide.
2. "U.S. and World Population Clock," US Census Bureau, accessed June 6, 2015, http://www.census.gov/popclock.
3. "The Human Heart: Blood Vessels," Franklin Institute, accessed June 6, 2015, http://learn.fi.edu/learn/heart/vessels/vessels.html.
4. Shannon Fischer, "What Lives in Your Belly Button? Study Finds 'Rain Forest' of Species," *National Geographic*, November 14, 2012, http://news.nationalgeographic.com/news/2012/11/121114-belly-button-bacteria-science-health-dunn/.
5. Josh Clark, "How Can Adrenaline Help You Lift a 3,500-pound Car?" *Threadgill Science* (blog), October 17, 2011, https://threadgillscience.wordpress.com/2011/10/17/how-can-adrenaline-help-you-lift-a-3500-pound-car-anatomy/.
6. Joseph Stromberg, "The Microscopic Structures of Dried Human Tears," Smithsonian.com, November 19, 2013, http://www.smithsonianmag.com/science-nature/the-microscopic-structures-of-dried-human-tears-180947766/?no-ist.
7. "New Oral Features Can Be Considered Unique as a Fingerprint," DentistryIQ, accessed June 24, 2015, http://www.dentistryiq.com

/articles/2014/01/new-oral-features-can-be-considered-unique-as-a-fingerprint.html.
8. Dr. Ben Kim, "Try Frequent Blinking for Healthier Eyes and Better Vision" (blog), March 13, 2014, http://drbenkim.com/blinking-healthy-eyes-vision.html.
9. Jordan S. Rubin, *The Maker's Diet for Weight Loss* (Lake Mary, FL: Charisma Media, 2008), 38.
10. "Get the Facts on Eating Disorders," National Eating Disorders Association, accessed June 7, 2015, http://www.nationaleatingdisorders.org/get-facts-eating-disorders.

Chapter 4

1. Susie Poppick, "Ten Subliminal Retail Tricks You're Probably Falling For," *Money*, December 3, 2014, http://time.com/money/3069933/ways-companies-trick-you-into-buying-more/.
2. Trent Hamm, "How Department Stores Trick You into Spending More," *The Simple Dollar*, April 5, 2007, updated September 17, 2014, http://www.thesimpledollar.com/15-ways-department-stores-try-to-trick-you-into-spending-more-than-you-need-to-and-10-ways-to-fight-back/.
3. Ibid.
4. "US Total Media Ad Spend Inches Up, Pushed by Digital," eMarketer, August 22, 2013, http://www.emarketer.com/Article/US-Total-Media-Ad-Spend-Inches-Up-Pushed-by-Digital/1010154.
5. Christina Austin, "The Billionaires' Club: Only 36 Companies Have $1,000 Million-Plus Ad Budgets," *Business Insider*, November 11, 2012, http://www.businessinsider.com/the-35-companies-that-spent-1-billion-on-ads-in-2011-2012-11?op=1.

Chapter 5

1. Maia Szalavitz, "The Secrets of Self-Control: The Marshmallow Test 40 Years Later," *Time*, September 6, 2011, http://healthland.time.com/2011/09/06/the-secrets-of-self-control-the-marshmallow-test-40-years-later/.

Chapter 6

1. "Resources for Speakers on Global Issues: Hunger; Vital Statistics," *United Nations*, accessed June 25, 2015, http://www.un.org/en/globalissues/briefingpapers/food/vitalstats.shtml.
2. Randy Alcorn, *Money, Possessions, and Eternity* (Carol Stream, IL: Tyndale, 2003), 291.
3. Amy Morin, "Seven Scientifically Proven Benefits of Gratitude That Will Motivate You to Give Thanks Year-Round," *Forbes*, November 23, 2014, http://www.forbes.com/sites/amymorin/2014/11/23/7-scientifically-proven-benefits-of-gratitude-that-will-motivate-you-to-give-thanks-year-round/.

Chapter 8

1. "Rotary Grater with Storage Device: US 20140014751 A1," "Patents," January 16, 2014, Google.com, accessed June 26, 2015, http://www.google.com/patents/US20140014751.

Chapter 9

1. Wireless Association, "Cell Phone Subscribers in the US, 1985–2010," Infoplease.com, accessed June 26, 2015, http://www.infoplease.com/ipa/A0933563.html.
2. "Internet Well on Way to Three Billion Users, UN Telecom Agency Reports," UN News Centre, May 5, 2014, accessed June 26, 2015, http://www.un.org/apps/news/story.asp?NewsID=47729#.VW8rkmbhL9I.

Chapter 10

1. "Facebook and Your Privacy," *Consumer Reports*, June 2012, accessed June 26, 2015, http://www.consumerreports.org/cro/magazine/2012/06/facebook-your-privacy/index.htm.

Chapter 12

1. Tamar Lewin, "If Your Kids Are Awake, They're Probably Online," *New York Times*, January 20, 2010, http://www.nytimes.com/2010/01/20/education/20wired.html?_r=0.

2. Jack Canfield, Mark Victor Hansen, and Kent Healy, *Chicken Soup for the Soul: Extraordinary Teens* (Cos Cob, CT: Chicken Soup for the Soul Publishing, 2009), 19–21.
3. *Chicken Soup for the Soul: Extraordinary Teens*, 83.